D0348410

# The French Lieutenant's Woman

## A SCREENPLAY

Other books by John Fowles

# The French Lieutenant's Woman
## A SCREENPLAY

In Memoriam

John Fowles - great modern British author.

Other books by Harold Pinter

BY

*HAROLD PINTER*

*With a foreword by* **John Fowles**

*Little, Brown and Company*      *Boston-Toronto*

COPYRIGHT © 1981 by United Artists Corporation

Foreword COPYRIGHT © 1981 by J. R. Fowles Ltd.

ALL RIGHTS RESERVED. NO PART OF THIS BOOK MAY BE REPRODUCED IN ANY FORM OR BY ANY ELECTRONIC OR MECHANICAL MEANS INCLUDING INFORMATION STORAGE AND RETRIEVAL SYSTEMS WITHOUT PERMISSION IN WRITING FROM THE PUBLISHER, EXCEPT BY A REVIEWER WHO MAY QUOTE BRIEF PASSAGES IN A REVIEW.

LIBRARY OF CONGRESS CATALOG CARD NO. 81-83032

FIRST EDITION

MV

PRINTED IN THE UNITED STATES OF AMERICA

The writing of this screenplay took over a year. This is the final version with which we began shooting. Inevitably a number of scenes were cut and some structural changes were made during the course of production.

*March 1981*                                    HAROLD PINTER

# The French Lieutenant's Woman

MERYL STREEP
JEREMY IRONS
A KAREL REISZ Film
"THE FRENCH LIEUTENANT'S WOMAN"
LEO McKERN
Screenplay by HAROLD PINTER
Based on the Novel by JOHN FOWLES
Music by CARL DAVIS
Produced by LEON CLORE
Directed by KAREL REISZ

United Artists
A Transamerica Company

Copyright © MCMLXXXI Juniper Films. All rights reserved.

# Contents

alas, he was the only part of it we truly wanted, and he very naturally declined to rat on his proposed partners. As with Karel, we felt we had forever lost our chance.

In 1978, almost a decade after that first approach and faced with the imminent collapse of yet another option, Tom went back to Karel; and at last fortune was kind to us. This time he said yes, with the one proviso that he could persuade Harold to tackle the script. Tom and I spent a fortnight on tenterhooks, while the two discussed possible solutions to all the problems. Then the second miracle happened: we found ourselves with the writer and director we most wanted. Further miracles were needed, and largely provided by the faith, tenacity and patience of Karel — and his leading actress and actor, Meryl Streep and Jeremy Irons — in the face of an unusually grim array of pre-production problems. But at last the day we had very nearly ceased to believe in did come to pass. On May 27, 1980, Karel stood beside his camera crew outside a country house near Lyme Regis, Sam the servant waited with a bunch of flowers on his starting-mark, and the magic word was said.

I most certainly mean no dispraise of the previous writers who did take the plunge if I say that none had succeeded. The chief stumbling-block was in any case one I have already suggested, and which no novelist can blame very sincerely — that of trying to remain faithful to the book. But *The French Lieutenant's Woman* was written at a time when I began to develop strong and perhaps idiosyncratic views on the proper domains of the cinema and the novel. There are of course large parts of those domains, since both media are essentially narrative, that overlap; yet there are others that are no-go territory . . . visual things the word can never capture (think, for instance, of the appalling paucity of vocabulary to define the endless nuances of facial expression), and word things the camera will never photograph nor actors ever speak.

Novels that consciously utilise this area forbidden to the film-maker (more anciently, to the illustrator) obviously pose very great problems; and the only likely result of 'being faithful' to such a book is a script spilling over with dialogue that is (through no fault of the screen-writer) really not dramatic dialogue at all, but an attempt to crush into a small valise all those long paragraphs of description, historical digression, character analysis and the rest that the vast portmanteau of novel form was specifically evolved to contain.

It is not only that language itself first arose to designate and 'show' things that could not be physically seen; the evolution of the novel, especially in our own century, and increasingly since the rise of structuralism and semiology (or a more exact knowledge of the nature of language and fictional text), has been more and more concerned with all those aspects of life and modes of feeling that can *never* be represented visually. It is not perhaps entirely chance that the invention of motion photography, this sudden great leap in our powers of exploring and imitating the outward of perception, coincided so exactly with the journey into inner space initiated by Freud and his compeers. The year 1895 saw not only the very first showing of the very first film but also the publication of *Studies in Hysteria*, that is, the birth of psycho-analysis.

This business of proper domains is one reason I am no longer in the least interested in scripting my own fiction. To assemble a book with a considerable and deliberate number of elements you know cannot be filmed, and then to disassemble and reconstruct it out of the elements that can, is surely an occupation best left to masochists or narcissists. Nowhere can there be a clearer case for a fresh and outside mind on the job. The second reason is that I know I am, like most novelists, far too corrupted by and addicted to the solitary freedoms of prose fiction (where the one megalomaniac plays producer, director, all the cast *and* camera) ever to be any good at a team art — or team anything, for that matter. The third reason is that true script-writers are a race apart in a craft apart. It is only vanity that makes other writers believe that anyone can turn a hand to it. I believed so myself, once. Then one day I persuaded Sidney Carroll to give me a copy of the superb scenario he wrote, with Robert Rossen, for *The Hustler*; and recognised (as I do again here) a league I shall never be in.

Another major problem with *The French Lieutenant's Woman* was what one critic called its stereoscopic vision, the fact that it is written from both a mid-Victorian and a modern viewpoint. None of the directors who worked on it ever wanted to dodge that 'diachronic' dilemma, though they came up with many different solutions. Nor, incidentally, did any of the producers.

As one studio head of production put it to me, he was profoundly uninterested in buying a latterday Victorian romance when there were hundreds of the genuine article — and from the most formidable corpus of writers in English fiction — lying about out of copyright and to be had for nothing.

A popular previous answer proposed an extension of a device used in the book, the creation of a character who was tacitly the author and also had a part in the Victorian story . . . someone who could both join the action from within and stand back and comment on it, rather as Anton Walbrook did in Max Ophuls' celebrated film, *La Ronde*. I never much fancied that, or only once. My path crossed Peter Ustinov's, in the unlikely setting of the Beverly Hills Hotel, and we spent an enjoyable evening discussing the idea. I best recall a wicked and marvellously mimicked series of anecdotes about a far more famous writer than either of us (and for whose work I had expressed too innocent an admiration). The scepticism about novelists' motives in general and the sending-up, through this one instance, of their public masks and private realities sold me lock, stock and barrel in the great raconteur's cause. He remains the only surrogate I could ever have borne in that role of author-ringmaster, had it ever survived discussion stage.

I am convinced now, in retrospect, that the only feasible answer was the one that Harold and Karel hit upon. We had all before been made blind to its existence by the more immediate problem of compressing an already dense and probably over-plotted book into two hours' screen time. The idea of adding an entirely new dimension and relationship to it would never have occurred to us; and quite reasonably so, with almost anyone but Harold Pinter.

I do not need to dwell on his universally acknowledged qualities as playwright, as creator of the kind of dialogue that can speak worlds in its smallest phrases, even in its silences, and not least as an issuer of the kind of challenge that every intelligent actor and actress likes to face. In those contexts this script speaks for itself. But his genius has a further string, and that seems to me to be his truly remarkable gift for reducing the long and complex without distortion. It may to the ignorant seem something of a negative or cutting-scissors skill, yet it is in fact infinitely valuable — and positive — in the cinema. The one practical advantage the novel factory (or novelist) has over his or her cinema equivalent lies in simplicity of production. The actual process of making a narrative film, however few the characters and simple the locations, is hideously complicated — and expensive; and the greatest gift a good screenwriter can give a director is not so much a version 'faithful' to the book as a version faithful to the very different production capability (and relation with audience) of the cinema.

I do not think of the present script as a mere 'version' of my novel; but as the blueprint (since of course this pudding's proof must lie finally in the seeing) of a brilliant metaphor for it. I approve entirely of this approach, and not only because I believe original authors have no right to interfere once they have got the scenarist and director they want, but even more because I am sure that viable transitions from the one medium to the other need just such an imaginative leap. Neither good film nor good novel has ever been made on a basis of safety. My same approval, I should add, went to the casting of an American actress in the title role. My liking for that possibility long ante-dated our good fortune in attracting Meryl Streep to the part, and for the same reason I have just mentioned: the metaphorical leap such a casting implies. In this particular case it also has for me a historical justice, since the principal freedom the heroine seeks is associated much more in my mind with nineteenth-century America than Victorian Britain. I suggested as much in the original novel.

If all novelists want is a literally faithful version of their books they should never in their right (or money-spurning) minds sell to the cinema. The longer the final cut, the more of the original they can hope to see; and if a literal fidelity is to be the criterion, the several hours a television serial can offer are manifestly superior to the miserable 110 minutes or so that distribution exigencies impose on the motion picture. I have heard filmmakers envy this luxury of time granted their television counterparts; but I suspect that in this they betray their own *métier*. The arbitrary limits imposed on film length are like those imposed on the dramatist by the physical stage, or on the poet by fixed form and metrical law. This is certainly one principal reason — in my view — why the cinema remains at its best a major art and television, except in very rare hands (like the late David Mercer's or Dennis Potter's), still dangerously close to a recording device, or mere translating machine.

I am often asked why I sell film rights at all, given the high risk of seeing nothing but a travesty as the end-product. It is a question I have invited, since in a later novel, *Daniel Martin*, I did not hide the contempt I feel for many aspects of the commercial cinema — or more exactly, since cost of production and mode of recoupment make all cinema more or less commercial, of the cinema where accountants reign, where profit comes first and everything else a long way after. This vile ethos was neatly exemplified in the main reason given by one studio when it turned down a forerunner of the present script. Its chief fault, we were informed, was that there was only one character with whom an American audience could happily identify . . . my little example of blind Victorian capitalism, the London store-owner, Mr Freeman. It was a nice question who was most insulted — the author, the director and screen-writer, or the studio-reader's fellow-countrymen. We decided in the end that it was, by several lengths, the last.

But for true cinema, cinema conceived and executed by artists as an art, or at least as a craft by sincere craftsmen, I have always had the greatest liking and respect. I have never had any belief in the notion that the cinema is 'killing' the novel (television is another matter, but even that has to do with the ubiquitous availability of reception, not with what is shown). The two ways of telling stories are much nearer sisters than anything else. A good director is always partly a novelist, and *vice versa* (and from long before the invention of photography). Quite apart from avowedly *auteur* cinema, the shared need to narrate, to create new worlds of character and atmosphere, to play the godgame, brings us incomparably closer than any other pairs of artists in different arts. It is the techniques that are so different, not the final aims; and if I have to justify (as rather an alarming number of readers have told me I must) the selling of rights, one reason certainly lies in my fascination with that difference of technique. Discovering its exact nature can be a very instructive experience for novelists, even when — perhaps, most of all when — the screened result disappoints.

The experience is also valuable in another way, one that may partly explain why some authors crave the literal fidelity I spoke about just now. Novelists have an almost archetypal fear that illustration will overstamp text, more precisely that their readers' imaginations (a vitally *creative* part in the total experience of the book) will be pinned down and manacled by a set of specific images. This began long before the cinema, of course. The harmony we may feel now between Dickens and his two great illustrators, Cruikshank and 'Phiz', certainly did not always exist at the time of creation. But it seems to me that this is a test, or challenge, the author is foolish to refuse — and even more foolish if, having accepted it, he or she tries to step over into another art and dictate how things are to be done there. It is particularly absurd in novelists, who are notoriously resentful of editorial interference in their own work.

If the text is worth its salt, it will survive being 'visualised'. If it meets its match, then word and image will marry, as has happened with Dickens, and enhance each other. If image does 'drown' text, then the latter was never going to survive, anyway. I was not amused (everyone else thought it hilariously funny) when a studio publicity man turned up in London during the present production and demanded to know why nothing had been done about the novelisation of Harold's script. But I took his general point: there is more than one way of telling a story, even inside the one medium, let alone in others. Risking the possibility that the film or television way turns out better, or will deeply change or colour how people respond to the literary way, is also a salutary experience; and one day someone will write a better novelisation than the film it is based on.

Cynics may think I am sliding over the most important reason: money. I am not so noble-minded I could deny that the money has its attractions; and I am not so modest I will not point out that rather more than my own bank-balance is involved. I have never seen a contemporary British novelist or playwright congratulated by government or industry for his or her contribution to foreign-currency earnings, job creation and so on; and I do not expect to do so, even though I doubt whether we are, Stakhanovite head for head, to be beaten in that particular race. It is true that we are only the indirect cause of the many millions of dollars that film productions of our work have brought into the post-war series of economies — all of which have failed miserably to support a national film industry. None the less, I think one has to be very sure indeed of one's motives before deciding that one's text is too precious a thing to be risked in the 'vulgarity' of a mass medium. What is really in the scales is not personal public image, or even personal financial reward, but work and wages for a lot of other people . . . and well beyond our ailing film industry proper.

But my chief private reason has to do with something else. Novelists are condemned to one of the loneliest professions in terms of work, and our wistful envy (the reverse of the coin of our megalomania) of those who work communally in the theatre, and now in the cinema, has a long record. I remember standing, that first day of shooting, with Harold and Karel during a break between takes, listening to them discuss some minor problem. I am sure it was the most banal and ordinary experience for them, but for me it was strange — as it has been strange on previous similar occasions. Words, all those endless rows of algebra on a page, are literally become flesh, have provoked this very actual presence, all this devotion, ingenuity, teamwork, skill with eye and ear. One has an odd sense of having come in for a moment from the cold. The strangeness was also, for me, this time, compounded by an unusual sense of trust. On 'first day', with a difficult project in a difficult medium, it could not have been anything to do with a certainty of the final-cut kind; but it had very much to do with a certainty that my two partners had done their best to achieve it.

That good moment at launching, in my philosophy of life just as important a thing as an eventually successful voyage, I owe, we all owe, to what follows. To a degree difficult to convey to the outsider, indeed to anyone who had not lived through ten years of abortive attempts, this script, this new keel, performed the final miracle. Quite simply, it at last made possible.

*January 1981*                                          JOHN FOWLES

# The French Lieutenant's Woman
## A SCREENPLAY

## 1. Exterior. The Cobb. Lyme Regis. Dawn. 1867.

*A clapperboard. On it is written:* THE FRENCH LIEUTENANT'S WOMAN. SCENE 1. TAKE 3.

*It shuts and withdraws, leaving a close shot of* ANNA, *the actress who plays* SARAH. *She is holding her hair in place against the wind.*

VOICE (off screen)

All right. Lets go.

*The actress nods, releases her hair. The wind catches it.*

VOICE (off screen)

Action.

SARAH *starts to walk along the Cobb, a stone pier in the Harbour of Lyme. It is dawn. Windy. Deserted. She is dressed in black. She reaches the end of the Cobb and stands still, staring out to sea.*

## 2. Interior. Hotel Room. The Cups. Hotel. Lyme. Day

CHARLES *sitting at a table, examining a fossil through a microscope. He is wearing a dressing gown and is whistling to himself.*

*Fossils lie on various shelves. A variety of scientific instruments and books are about the room.*

CHARLES *stops, looks up, considers, and suddenly calls:*

CHARLES

Sam!

*He turns.*

Sam!

*He mutters.*

Where the devil is he?

*He stands and goes to the window.*

## 3. Exterior Lyme High St. Charles' P.O.V.

*The High Street at early morning. Men on horse-back. A shepherd with a flock of sheep. A street market. In background Lyme Bay.*

## 4. Interior. Hotel room.

CHARLES *picks up a telescope and looks through it out of the window.*

## 5. The street market. Charles' P.O.V.

*The telescope moves through sheep and people to focus finally on* SAM, *who is standing by a flower stall. He holds a bunch of flowers. He is talking to a young girl. He gives her a flower. She giggles, and turns away.*

## 6. Close up. Charles watching.

## 7. Exterior. The street.

SAM *walking between horses, and treading with distaste over horse dung, the bunch of flowers in his hand.*
CHARLES' *voice over.*

> CHARLES
>
> Sam!

> SAM *looks up.*

## 8. Exterior. The Cups Hotel.

CHARLES *at his window.*

> CHARLES
>
> Come up here!

> SAM
>
> At the double, sir.

## 9. Interior. Hotel Room. Day.

CHARLES *dips his shaving brush in a bowl and begins to lather his face.*
SAM *enters.*

> SAM
>
> Sir?

> CHARLES
>
> Where the devil have you been?

> SAM
>
> I was just taking the flowers up to the house, sir, as you –

> CHARLES
>
> Change of plan. I'll want my grey suit.

SAM

Your grey suit? But I thought you were going fossilling this morning, sir.

CHARLES

No fossils today, Sam. Today is a day for action.

SAM

Yes, sir.

CHARLES

I shall do it this morning, immediately after breakfast!

SAM

Do what, sir?

CHARLES

I should have done it weeks ago.

SAM

Ah. Well better late than never, sir.

*SAM picks up the razor.*

*CHARLES takes it from him.*

CHARLES

I'll shave myself this morning. Breakfast! A double dose of muffins. And kidneys and liver and bacon.

*SAM goes to the door.*

And Sam!

SAM

Mr. Charles?

CHARLES

When we get there be sure you don't dally with Miss Ernestina's maid.

SAM

Me, sir? Dally, sir?

CHARLES

This is my day, not yours.

*SAM goes out. CHARLES looks at himself in the mirror, shaves.*


**10.  Exterior. Street. Lyme. Day.**

*Carriage, with CHARLES and SAM in it, going up hill along the High Street.*

**11. Exterior. Country lane. Day.**
*The carriage out of Lyme and into open landscape.*

**12. Exterior. Mrs. Tranter's house. Day.**
*The carriage arrives.* CHARLES *jumps out, strides to the front door. It is opened at once by* MARY.
> MARY
Good morning, sir.
> CHARLES
Good morning. Please tell your mistress I would like to see her. Ah! Mrs. Tranter!
*He takes off his hat and walks in.*
MARY *remains at the door for a moment, looking for* SAM.

**13. Sam winking at Mary.**

**14. Interior. Mrs. Tranter's house. Hall.**
MRS. TRANTER *walks towards* CHARLES.
> MRS. TRANTER
Charles! My goodness, you are up early!
> CHARLES
Good morning Mrs. Tranter. A beautiful morning.
> MRS. TRANTER
It is indeed.
> CHARLES
Is Ernestina . . . awake?
> MRS. TRANTER
Mary, is my niece awake? .
> MARY
She is, mu'm.
> MRS. TRANTER
Tell her Mr. Charles is here.
> MARY
Yes, mu'm.
MARY *bobs and goes up the stairs.*
> CHARLES
Might it be possible for me to see Ernestina . . . alone?

4

## 15.    Interior. Staircase.

MARY *stops and looks down into the hall.*

MRS. TRANTER

But of course. Of course.

*She leads* CHARLES *towards the garden room.*
MARY *turns quickly and hurries up the stairs.*

## 16.    Interior. Ernestina's bedroom.

ERNESTINA *half dressed.* MARY *knocks and enters.*

MARY

Mr. Charles is here, Miss, to see you.

ERNESTINA

Mr. Charles?

MARY

He's downstairs waiting for you Miss. He wants to
speak to you.

ERNESTINA

Oh, dear! What shall I . . . What dress shall I wear?

MARY

Oh your green is so lovely Miss. You look as pretty
as a picture in your green.

ERNESTINA

Yes, yes. My green. I'll wear that.

## 17.    Interior. Living room.

MRS. TRANTER

The conservatory . . . is a private place. Will that
suit?

CHARLES

It will suit. Thank you. I shall wait for her . . . in the
conservatory.

## 18.    Interior. Kitchen.

*The* COOK *at the sink.*

SAM *at the window, looking across the garden into the
conservatory.* CHARLES' *figure can be discerned, walking
about.*

COOK

I always thought you from London spent half the
day in bed.

5

SAM

No ma'm. Up and about, we're always up and about, early birds ready to catch the early worm, ma'm. Us Londoners.

ERNESTINA *can be seen going into the conservatory.*
MARY *comes into the kitchen.*

SAM

She's gone in to him.

MARY

Doesn't she look a princess?

COOK

What's going on in this house this morning?

## 19. Interior. Living room.

MRS. TRANTER *looking at* ERNESTINA *and* CHARLES *through the conservatory window.* CHARLES *is talking.*

## 20. Interior. Conservatory. Day.

CHARLES

Ernestina, it cannot have escaped your notice that it is fully six weeks since I came down here to Lyme from London.

ERNESTINA

No. It has not escaped my notice.

CHARLES *clears his throat.*

CHARLES

I came to Lyme to explore the flint beds of the Undercliff, to look for fossils – but I have stayed for you.

ERNESTINA

Ah!

CHARLES

For your sweet company.

ERNESTINA

Thank you.

## 21. Interior. Ernestina's bedroom. Day.

MRS. TRANTER *tiptoes in. She moves to the window from which she can see the conservatory below.*

## 22.  Interior. Kitchen.

SAM

She's not going to turn him down, is she?

MARY

Never. She'd give her left arm. *And* all her dresses.


## 23.  Interior. Conservatory.

CHARLES

I am here this morning to enquire if you would allow me to ask your father . . . for your hand.
*She looks at him.*

ERNESTINA

Yes. I would allow it.

CHARLES (*with a smile*)

Mind you, I don't know that he approves of me. After all, I don't do what he considers to be work.

ERNESTINA

Are you suggesting that it is entirely Papa's decision?

CHARLES

Oh no. It is yours.

ERNESTINA

Yes. It is. Papa will do what I want.

CHARLES

In that case . . . might you take pity on a crusty old scientist, who holds you very dear . . . and marry me?
ERNESTINA *bursts into tears.*

ERNESTINA

Oh Charles! I have waited so long for this moment.
*He takes her hands.*


## 24.  Interior. Kitchen.

SAM

He's home and dry.


## 25.  Interior. Ernestina's bedroom.

MRS. TRANTER *watching, delighted, her hand to her mouth.*

7

## 26. Interior. Conservatory.

CHARLES *under an overhanging branch.*

CHARLES

This is not mistletoe, but it will do.

ERNESTINA

Oh Charles . . .

*They kiss chastely.*

## 27. Hotel room. Early morning. Present. 1979.

*Dim light. A man and a woman in bed asleep. It is at once clear that they are the man and woman playing* CHARLES *and* SARAH, *but we do not immediately appreciate that the time is the present.*

*A telephone rings.*

MIKE *turns, lifts receiver.*

MIKE

Yes? (*Pause.*) Who is it? (*Pause.*) Yes, it is. (*Pause.*) I'll tell her.

MIKE *puts the phone down, turns on light, wakes* ANNA.

MIKE

Anna.

ANNA

Mmmn?

MIKE

You're late. They're waiting for you.

ANNA

Oh God.

*She sits up.*

What happened to the wake-up call?

MIKE

I don't know.

ANNA (*yawning*)

Who called?

MIKE

Jack.

*She looks at him.*

ANNA

Did you answer the phone?

MIKE

Yes.

ANNA

But then – they'll know you're in my room, they'll all know.

MIKE

In your bed.
*He kisses her.*
I want them to know.

ANNA

Christ, look at the time.
*He holds her.*

ANNA

They'll fire me for immorality.
*He embraces her.*
They'll think I'm a whore.

MIKE

You are.


**28. Exterior. Hotel. Present.**

ANNA *getting into car. It drives off.*


**29. Interior. Car.**

ANNA *sitting.*

CHAUFFEUR

Chilly morning.


**30. Interior. Small cottage. Lyme. Day.**

*Two labourers are carrying a coffin down the stairs. They have difficulty manoeuvering it.*
*They pass the sitting figure of* SARAH *and carry the coffin into the street, leaving the door open.*
SARAH *is sitting by the window, drawing.*


**31. Close up. The drawing.**

*The drawing is of an old woman on her death bed.*


**32. Interior. Cottage.**

*The* VICAR's *voice is heard giving instructions to the labourers. He comes into the room. He looks down at* SARAH. *She continues to draw.*

9

VICAR

You realise you cannot stay here any longer? I happen to know that Miss Duff has made no provision for you in her will. The place is to be sold.
   *Pause.*
How much money do you possess?
   *Pause.*

VICAR

When did you last eat?
   *Pause.*
Miss Woodruff, I think I know someone who can help you. Mrs. Poulteney from the Grange. She might take you in.
   SARAH *looks up.*

SARAH

Does her house overlook the sea?

VICAR

It does. Yes.

SARAH

Then I would be grateful for your good offices, Vicar.


33.   **Exterior. Mr. Freeman's wharf. Port of London. Day.**
   *A carriage draws up.* CHARLES *gets out of it and looks about him. A ship unloading. Tea chests, on pulleys, being deposited on the wharf. They are stamped: 'Freeman's Teas'. Men wheeling the tea chests towards the warehouse. Dray horses with carts standing by.*


34.   **Interior. Mr. Freeman's office. Warehouse. Day.**
   *The office looks over the wharf.* MR. FREEMAN *and* CHARLES *are sitting at his desk.*

MR. FREEMAN

Yes, indeed. I recognise, Charles, that you bring to Ernestina not only your love and protection, but also . . . in time . . . a considerable inheritance.

CHARLES

That is so.

10

MR. FREEMAN

I know my daughter loves you. You seem to me an upright man. Let us shake hands.

*They stand and shake hands.* MR. FREEMAN *clasps* CHARLES' *shoulder warmly.*

I started here, Charles, with my dear wife at my side.

*He looks up at a portrait of Mrs. Freeman.* CHARLES, *too, looks up.*


35. **Interior. Mr. Freeman's Warehouse. Day.**

*A large body of men stacking tea chests as they arrive from the wharf.* MR. FREEMAN *and* CHARLES *walk through the warehouse.*

MR. FREEMAN

We could have met at my office in the City, but I thought you would be interested to see this place.

CHARLES

Indeed I am.

MR. FREEMAN

In a few months we shall be opening depots in Bristol and Liverpool.

*They walk out onto the wharf.*


36. **Exterior. The wharf. Day.**

*The ship unloading.*

MR. FREEMAN *and* CHARLES *survey the scene.*

MR. FREEMAN

You know I have no son, Charles?

CHARLES

I do, sir, yes.

MR. FREEMAN

This isn't the time to talk about it, but if you ever felt disposed to explore the world of commerce, I would be delighted to be your guide.

CHARLES *looks at him.*

CHARLES

Thank you.

MR. FREEMAN

The times are on our side. This is the age of progress, Charles. Progress is like a lively horse. Either you collar it or you come a cropper. I am convinced that one day an empire of sorts will come to Ernestina and yourself. And thereafter to your children.

## 37. Exterior. The Cobb. Lower level. Lyme. Day.

CHARLES *and* ERNESTINA *walking towards the camera.*

ERNESTINA

Oh dear, don't tell me. Did he talk of his famous 'empire'?

CHARLES

He did.

ERNESTINA

And did he propose that you might one day join him in the ruling of it?

CHARLES

He was most respectful of what he called my position as a 'scientist and a gentleman'. In fact he asked me about my . . . my work. But as I didn't think fossils were his line exactly, I gave him a brief discourse on the Theory of Evolution instead.

ERNESTINA

How wicked of you!

CHARLES

Yes. He didn't seem to think very much of it, I must admit. In fact he ventured the opinion that Mr. Darwin should be exhibited in a cage in the zoological gardens. In the monkey house.

CHARLES *stops walking. A gust of wind. They are near the steps to the upper level of the Cobb.*

The wind is very strong. Shall we return?

*He suddenly sees* SARAH *standing at the very end of the Cobb, looking out to sea. The wind blows her shawl.*

Good Lord! What on earth is she doing?

ERNESTINA

Who is it?

CHARLES

I don't know.

ERNESTINA *peers at the woman.*

ERNESTINA

Oh, it's poor 'Tragedy'.

CHARLES

Tragedy?

ERNESTINA

One of her nicknames. The fishermen have a grosser name for her.

CHARLES

What?

ERNESTINA

They call her the French Lieutenant's . . .

*She looks at him.*

. . . Woman.

CHARLES

Do they?

*A stronger gust of wind. The woman sways, clutches a cannon bollard.*

I must speak to her. She could fall. (*To* ERNESTINA:) Please wait for me.

ERNESTINA

She won't thank you. She's mad.

CHARLES

It's dangerous.

CHARLES *climbs the steps to the upper ledge of the Cobb and runs towards* SARAH.

Madam!

*The woman does not turn.*

CHARLES *speaks loudly above the wind and sea.*

Forgive me, I am alarmed for your safety. The wind –

*She turns sharply, stares at him. He stops speaking.*

## 38. Close up. Sarah. Staring at him.

## 39. Exterior. The Cobb. Long shot. Day.

CHARLES *and* SARAH, *staring at each other.*

13

**40.  Interior. Mrs. Tranter's house. Kitchen. Day.**
MARY *setting sandwiches and cakes on a tray.*
SAM *approaches her from behind, squeezes her waist.*
*The servants' bell rings.*

MARY
They want their tea.

SAM
Let them wait.

MARY
Don't be silly.

SAM
You don't want to spoil them.
*He tickles her. She giggles.*
*The bell rings again.*


**41.  Interior. Ernestina's sitting room. Day.**
ERNESTINA *at bell pull.* CHARLES *is looking out of the window.*

ERNESTINA
What *is* she doing? I'm dying for my tea.

CHARLES
Tell me, who is this French Lieutenant?

ERNESTINA
Oh . . . he is a man she is said to have . . .

CHARLES
Fallen in love with?

ERNESTINA
Worse than that.

CHARLES
Ah. And he abandoned her? Is there a child?

ERNESTINA
I think not. Oh, it's all gossip.

CHARLES
What is she doing here?

ERNESTINA
They say she is waiting for him to return.
ERNESTINA *goes to the bell pull and pulls it.*

CHARLES
How banal.

14

**42. Interior. Kitchen.**

*The bell ringing.*

MARY *trying to get away from* SAM's *embrace.*

MARY

Stop it!

**43. Interior. Sitting room.**

ERNESTINA

Where *is* the girl? It's probably your man making eyes at her.

CHARLES

Out of the question. My man is a true gentleman's gentleman.

ERNESTINA

Huh!

CHARLES

But how does she live?

ERNESTINA

Who?

CHARLES

This . . . French Lieutenant's Woman.

ERNESTINA

She sews, or something. Oh, really, I don't want to talk about her.

**44. Exterior. Mrs. Poulteney's. Evening.**

SARAH *walking alone on a country path towards* MRS. POULTENEY's *house.*

**45. Interior. Mrs. Poulteney's house. Window in hall. Day.**

SARAH *standing, looking out of window.*
*Servants on stairs watch her.*
MR. FAIRLEY *passes her, without a glance.*
*From the landing the* VICAR's *voice.*

VICAR

Miss Woodruff, would you please come up?

SARAH *climbs the stairs, past the servants. The* VICAR
*is waiting at the door of* MRS. POULTENEY's *room.*

Do come in.

15

## 46. Interior. Mrs. Poulteney's sitting room.

MRS. POULTENEY *is sitting*.

VICAR

Mrs. Poulteney, this is Miss Woodruff.

MRS. POULTENEY

Ah. I see.

*She studies her.*

I wish, as the Vicar has told you, to take a companion. The Vicar has indicated to me that you might be a suitable person for such a post. You are without employment?

SARAH

I am, ma'm.

MRS. POULTENEY

But you have education? You have been a governess?

SARAH

I have, ma'm.

MRS. POULTENEY

The post of companion requires a person of irreproachable moral character. I have my servants to consider.

*The VICAR coughs.*

MRS. POULTENEY *looks at him and then turns back to regard* SARAH *in silence.*

You speak French, I believe?

SARAH

I do, ma'm.

MRS. POULTENEY

I do not like the French.

*The VICAR coughs again.*

Perhaps you might leave us now, Mr. Forsythe?

VICAR

Yes, of course, Mrs. Poulteney.

*He stands and bows.*

Good afternoon.

*He leaves the room.*

MRS. POULTENEY

Mr. Forsythe informs me that you retain an attachment to a . . . foreign person.

16

SARAH

I do not wish to speak of it, ma'm.

MRS. POULTENEY *stares at her.*

MRS. POULTENEY

But what if this person returns. What then?

SARAH *bows her head and shakes it.*

You shake your head, but I have heard, from the most impeccable witnesses, that you are always to be seen at the same place when you are out. You stand on the Cobb and look to sea.

SARAH *looks at her.*

I have been encouraged to believe that you are in a state of repentance, but I must emphasise that such staring out to sea is provocative, intolerable and sinful.

SARAH

Do you wish me to leave the house, Mrs. Poulteney?

MRS. POULTENEY

I wish you to show that this . . . person is expunged from your heart.

SARAH

How am I to show it?

MRS. POULTENEY

By not exhibiting your shame.

*Pause.*

SARAH

I will do as you wish, ma'm.

MRS. POULTENEY

I will not have French books in my house.

SARAH

I possess none.

MRS. POULTENEY

I would like to hear you read from the Bible. If your expression is agreeable to me, you shall have the position.

*She hands* SARAH *a Bible.*

17

**47.  Interior. Dressing room. Present.**

> ANNA *is standing in her corset, her back to the camera. Her dresser is unlacing the corset. It comes off.* ANNA *rubs her waist. She sighs with relief.*

ANNA

Christ!


**48.  Interior. Mrs. Poulteney's sitting room. Evening.**

> MRS. POULTENEY *and* SARAH, *in different dresses, sitting.* SARAH *is reading from the Bible: Psalm 140.*

SARAH

Deliver me, O Lord, from the evil man;
Preserve me from the violent man;
Which imagine mischiefs in their heart;
Continually are they gathered for war;
They have sharpened their tongues like a serpent;
Adders' poison is under their lip. Selah.
Keep me, O Lord, from the hands of the wicked;
Preserve me from the violent man,
Who have purposed to overthrow my goings.

> SARAH *looks at* MRS. POULTENEY, *who has fallen asleep.*


**49.  Interior. Mike's hotel room. Lyme. Day. Present.**

> ANNA, *with glasses on, reading a book.* MIKE *reading the sports page of a newspaper. She looks up.*

ANNA

Wow!

MIKE

What?

ANNA (*referring to the book*)

Listen to this.
'In 1857 the Lancet estimated that there were eighty thousand prostitutes in the County of London. Out of every sixty houses one was a brothel.'

MIKE

Mmm.
> *Pause.*

18

ANNA (*reading*)
'We reach the surprising conclusion that at a time when the male population of London of all ages was one and a quarter million, the prostitutes were receiving clients at a rate of two million per week.'

MIKE
Two million!

ANNA
You know when I say − in the graveyard scene − about going to London? Wait.
*She picks up her script of* The French Lieutenant's Woman, *flips the pages, finds the page. She reads aloud:*
'If I went to London I know what I should become. I should become what some already call me in Lyme'.

MIKE
Yes?

ANNA
Well, that's what she's really faced with.

*She picks up the book.*

This man says that hundreds of the prostitutes were nice girls like governesses who had lost their jobs. See what I mean? You offend your boss, you lose your job. That's it! You're on the streets. I mean, it's real.
MIKE *has picked up a calculator and starts tapping out figures.*

MIKE
The male population was a million and a quarter but the prostitutes had two million clients a week?

ANNA
Yes. That's what he says.

MIKE
Allow about a third off for boys and old men . . . That means that outside marriage − a Victorian gentleman had about two point four fucks a week.
*She looks at him.*

## 50.  Exterior. Lyme. Day.
*Near the Cobb. A helicopter takes off.*

## 51.  Interior. Helicopter.
MIKE *sits beside the pilot.*
*They speak, pointing at the ground but we do not hear their words.*

## 52.  Exterior. Undercliff from helicopter. Day.
*Travelling eye-line from helicopter.*
*The viewpoint, at first at sea level, swoops dramatically up from the rocks of the falling coast-line to a high view of the vast wilderness of the Undercliff.*

## 53.  Exterior. Undercliff. Day.
*The Undercliff is a great dense wood inland of the cliffs, looking over Lyme Bay. It has a very strange atmosphere, quite un-English in character. The terrain is abrupt, cut by deep chasms and towers of chalk and flint cliffs. The undergrowth is matted, the foliage lush. The ashes and beech trees are vast and tangled. Chasms are choked with ivy and wild clematis. The bracken is eight feet tall. Masses of wild flowers.*
CHARLES, *dressed in his fossil-hunting clothes, and carrying equipment, stands looking up at the vast trees above him.*

## 54.  Charles seen, from high, through trees.

## 55.  Hammer on flint.
*The camera tracks back to reveal* CHARLES *at the bottom of an inland flint cliff, hammering.*
*He puts hammer down, takes out chisel, begins to scrape the surface. He puts chisel down, drinks from water-bottle, cools his forehead with water. He is about to pick up chisel when he looks down sharply.*

## 56.  The trees. Charles' P.O.V.
*A figure glimpsed, moving through trees.*

**57. Charles lifting small telescope.**

**58. The trees, magnified.**
*Stillness.*

**59. Undercliff.**
CHARLES *leaves the flint cliff. He looks at the place where he had glimpsed the figure. He hesitates, and then goes towards the trees.*
*He tramps through the matted undergrowth, suddenly falls. He stands. He goes on. Branches claw at him.*
*He suddenly finds a path. He follows it.*
*It opens onto a little green plateau, studded with wild-flowers.*
*He is close to the edge of the Undercliff.*

**60. Lyme Bay far below.**

**61. Charles on the plateau.**
*The plateau goes to a brink. He walks towards it and looks down.*

**62. The ledge.**
*On the broad sloping ledge of grass* SARAH *is sitting. The ledge is five feet below the plateau. Below it is a mass of brambles – beyond it the cliff falling to the sea.*

**63. The plateau.**
CHARLES *looking down.*

**64. The ledge.**
SARAH *sitting on the ledge, looking out to sea. She turns sharply, and sees* CHARLES.
*She stands quickly, stares at him.*

**65. Charles and Sarah.**
CHARLES
I am very sorry to disturb you.
*He turns and climbs back towards the path.*

**66. Close up. Anna. Caravan. Present.**

*She takes off her wig, puts it on a table. She shakes her hair loose. She stares at her face in the mirror.*

**67. Exterior. The dairy.**

CHARLES *seen emerging from trees. He walks towards the dairy. The dairy woman sitting by the door. She looks up as he approaches.*

**68. Interior. Mrs. Tranter's house. Day.**

MARY *opening the front door.* SAM *stands on the doorstep with a bunch of flowers.*

                   SAM

For the lovely young lady upstairs.

*He gives the flowers to* MARY *and brings a small posy from behind his back.*

And for the even more lovely one down.

*He gives the posy to her. She smells the flowers and looks at him through them.*

**69. Exterior. Dairy.**

*The* DAIRYWOMAN *is ladling milk from a churn into a china bowl.* CHARLES *receives it and drinks.*

*The* DAIRYMAN *comes out of the door; a vast bald man. The woman disappears. The man stares.*

                 CHARLES

Very fine milk.

*The man stares.*

How much do I owe you?

                DAIRYMAN

A penny.

CHARLES *gives him a penny.*

                 CHARLES

Thank you very much.

*Suddenly a figure in black appears out of the trees walking on the path towards Lyme. It is* SARAH. *She glances in their direction and goes on. The two men watch her.*

Do you know that lady?

DAIRYMAN

Aye.

CHARLES

Does she come this way often?

DAIRYMAN

Often enough. And she been't no lady. She be the French Loot'n'nt's Whore.

CHARLES *glares at him.*


70.  Interior. Ernestina's room. Day.

*A knock at the door.* MARY *comes in, with flowers.*

MARY

From Mr. Charles, Miss Tina. With his compliments.

ERNESTINA

Did he bring them himself?

MARY

No, miss.

ERNESTINA

Where is Mr. Charles?

MARY

Don't know, miss. I didn't ask him.

ERNESTINA

Ask who?

MARY

His servant, miss.

ERNESTINA

But I heard you speak with him.

MARY

Yes, miss.

ERNESTINA

What about?

MARY

Oh just the time of day, miss.

ERNESTINA

You will kindly remember that he comes from London.

MARY

Yes, miss.

23

ERNESTINA

If he makes advances I wish to be told at once. Now
bring me some barley water.
*Sullenly* MARY *bobs a curtsey and leaves the room.*
ERNESTINA *takes envelope from flowers and opens it.*

## 71. The letter.

'*For my beloved. Charles.*'

## 72. Exterior. Undercliff.

SARAH *walking.*
CHARLES *pursuing her. He catches her up.*

CHARLES

Madam!
SARAH *stops, turns to him.*
*He smiles.*

CHARLES

I am very sorry to have disturbed you just now.
*She inclines her head, moves on. He walks with her.*
I gather you have recently become . . . secretary to
Mrs. Poulteney. May I accompany you? Since we
walk in the same direction?
*She stops.*

SARAH

I prefer to walk alone.
*They stand.*

CHARLES

May I introduce myself?

SARAH

I know who you are.

CHARLES

Ah . . . then?

SARAH

Kindly allow me to go on my way alone.
*Pause.*
And please tell no–one you have seen me in this
place.
*She walks on.*
*He remains still, looking after her.*

**73. Interior. Caravan. Present. Day.**

ANNA *in her caravan. A knock on the door.*

ANNA

Hello!

MIKE *comes in.*

MIKE

May I introduce myself?

ANNA

I know who you are.

*They smile. He closes the door.*

MIKE

So you prefer to walk alone?

ANNA

Me? Not me. Her.

MIKE

I enjoyed that.

ANNA

What?

MIKE

Our exchange. Out there.

ANNA

Did you? I never know . . .

MIKE

Know what?

ANNA

Whether it's any good.

MIKE

Listen. Do you find me – ?

ANNA

What?

MIKE

Sympathetic.

ANNA

Mmn. Definitely.

MIKE

I don't mean me. I mean him.

ANNA

Definitely.

MIKE

But you still prefer to walk alone?

ANNA

Who? Me – or her?

MIKE

Her. You like company.
*He strokes the back of her neck.*
Don't you?

ANNA *(smiling)*

Not always. Sometimes I prefer to walk alone.

MIKE

Tell me, when you said that – outside – you swished your
skirt – very provocative. Did you mean it?

ANNA

Well, it worked. Didn't it?
THIRD ASSISTANT*'s face at door.*

THIRD ASSISTANT

We're going again.

## 74.   Exterior. Undercliff. Day. Another angle.

CHARLES

May I accompany you? Since we walk in the same
direction?
*She stops.*

SARAH

I prefer to walk alone.

CHARLES

May I introduce myself?

SARAH

I know who you are.
*She collapses in laughter. He grins.*

VOICE *(off screen)*

Cut! *(With bewilderment.)* What's going on?

## 75.   Interior. Mrs. Poulteney's sitting room. Day.

MRS. POULTENEY *is sitting.* SARAH *standing.* MRS
POULTENEY *is looking away from* SARAH.

MRS. POULTENEY

I should never have listened to the Vicar. I should
have listened to the dictates of my own common
sense. You are a cunning, wicked creature.
*Pause.*

26

SARAH

May I know of what I am accused?

MRS. POULTENEY *turns sharply to her.*

MRS. POULTENEY

You have been seen walking on the Undercliff!
Not twice, but thrice!

SARAH

But what, pray, is the sin in that?

MRS. POULTENEY

The sin! You, a young woman, alone, in such a
place!

SARAH

It is nothing but a large wood.

MRS. POULTENEY

I know very well what it is. And what goes on there
– the sort of person who frequents it.

SARAH

No-one frequents it. I go there to be alone.

MRS. POULTENEY

Do you contradict me, Miss? Am I not to know
what I speak of?

*Pause.*

I will permit no-one in my employ to go to or to be
seen near, that place. You will confine your walks
to where it is seemly. Do I make myself clear?

SARAH

Yes. I am to walk in the paths of righteousness.

MRS. POULTENEY *looks at her sharply.*


76.  **Interior. Mrs. Tranter's house. Kitchen. Day.**

MARY *bustling about the kitchen.* SAM, *with his feet up,*
*watching her.*

SAM

Why don't you come with the young lady, when
they're married, as her maid?

MARY

I'm Mrs. Tranter's maid.

27

She wouldn't mind.
*He stands and moves to her.*
I could show you around London, see the sights.
MARY
You wouldn't want to go walking out with me in
London, with all them fashionable London girls.
SAM
If you had the clothes, you'd do. You'd do very
nice.
*She moves away.*
MARY
You're joking with me.
SAM
I'm dead serious. I'm not going to stay a servant all
my life. Not by a long chalk. I'm going to be a
draper. I want my own shop.
*She looks at him wide-eyed.*
All I need is one hundred pounds.
MARY
And where are you going to get that?
SAM
I'll get it.
*He takes her face in his hands, kisses her, murmurs
softly:*
I'll get it.

## 77. Interior. Ernestina's sitting room. Day.

ERNESTINA *is lying on a chaise longue wearing a peignoir.*
CHARLES *is kissing her hand.*
ERNESTINA
You shall not have a drop of tea until you have
accounted for every moment of your day.
CHARLES *brings from behind his back a fossil and gives
it to her.*
CHARLES
A gift – for you.
ERNESTINA
Good gracious! How pretty. What is it?

28

CHARLES

An echinoderm. It was once a sea urchin, of sorts.
Micraster Coranguinium.

ERNESTINA

Where did you find it?

CHARLES

I have been exploring the Undercliff.

ERNESTINA

The Undercliff? But it's supposed to be dangerous
and disreputable. The only people who go there
. . . are servants.

CHARLES

And why do they go there?

ERNESTINA

I hear they go there . . . to dally.

CHARLES

Do they indeed?
Well, I saw no dallying servants.

ERNESTINA

Nor dallying scientists?

CHARLES (*smiling*)

No.
*Pause.*

ERNESTINA

You don't intend to take me there, I hope.

CHARLES

Certainly not. The place is full of wild and ferocious
animals. I wouldn't want you eaten up.
*She takes his hand.*

ERNESTINA

Charles . . . please tell me . . . do you think me very
foolish? You see, I'm so little educated. But I am a
person of feeling.
*He squeezes her hand.*

CHARLES

You are a person of sweet feeling.


**78. Interior. Hotel. Empty billiard room. Night. Present.**

MIKE *and* ANNA *rehearsing, holding scripts.*

MIKE

Miss Woodruff!

ANNA

Just a minute, I've lost the place.
*She turns pages of script.*

MIKE

I suddenly see you. You've got your coat caught in brambles. I see you, then you see me. We look at each other, then I say: 'Miss Woodruff'.

ANNA

All right.

MIKE

Right. I see you. Get your coat caught in the bramble.
*She mimes her coat caught in bramble.*

MIKE

Right. Now I'm looking at you.
You see me. Look at me.

ANNA

I am.

MIKE

Miss Woodruff!

ANNA

I'm looking at you.

MIKE

Yes, but now you come towards me, to pass me. It's a narrow path, muddy.
*She walks towards him.*
You slip in the mud.

ANNA

Whoops!
*She falls.*

MIKE

Beautiful. Now I have to help you up.

ANNA

Let's start over again.
*She goes back to the chair.*
I've got my coat caught in the brambles.
Suddenly you see me. Then I see you.

MIKE

Miss Woodruff!

30

*She mimes her coat caught in brambles, tugs at it, walks along carpet towards him. He steps aside. She moves swiftly to pass him, and slips. She falls to her knees. He bends to help her up. She looks up at him. He stops a moment, looking down, and then gently lifts her. With his hand on her elbow, he leads her towards the window.*

I dread to think, Miss Woodruff, what would happen if you should one day turn your ankle in a place like this.

*She is silent, looking down.*

*He looks down at her face, her mouth.*

ANNA

I must . . . go back.

MIKE

Will you permit me to say something first? I know I am a stranger to you, but —

*Sharp cut to:*

## 79. Sarah turning sharply. A branch snapping.

## 80. Undercliff. Day.

*Men's low voices.*

CHARLES *standing.* SARAH *moving swiftly over the grass and disappearing behind a thicket of gorse.*

*The voices come nearer. Suddenly a dog and two men appear, in the undergrowth. The dog barks, the men stare at* CHARLES *and then withdraw hurriedly. Racing footsteps; a shrill whistle; the dog turns and disappears after the men. Silence.*

## 81. The thicket of gorse.

SARAH *stands, tensely.*

CHARLES *appears.*

*The gorse is in full bloom. He studies her standing against it.*

CHARLES

It was not really necessary to hide.

SARAH

No gentleman who cares for his good name can be seen with the scarlet woman of Lyme.

31

CHARLES

Miss Woodruff, I know something . . . about your circumstances. It cannot be . . . any great pleasure to be in Mrs. Poulteney's employ.

*She does not respond.*

You should leave Lyme. I understand you have excellent qualifications.

SARAH

I cannot leave this place.

CHARLES

Why? You have no family ties, I believe, that confine you to Dorset?

SARAH

I have ties.

CHARLES

To this French gentleman?

*She turns away.*

Permit me to insist. These matters are like wounds. If no-one dares speak of them, they fester. If he does not return, he was not worthy of you. If he returns –

SARAH

He will never return.

*Pause.*

CHARLES

You fear he will never return?

SARAH

I know he will never return.

CHARLES

I do not take your meaning.

*She looks away, stays silent, looks back at him.*
*She speaks calmly, looking into his eyes.*

SARAH

He is married.

## 82. Mrs. Tranter's house. Kitchen. Day.

*The* COOK *and* UNDERMAID *preparing a tray of tea.* SAM *sitting.* MARY *enters.*

SAM

Who is it?

MARY

It's that Mrs. Poulteney. The one who kicked me
out onto the street.

SAM

Is it? Poison her tea.

MARY

I'm not frightened of her. I work here now, where
I'm respected.

SAM

I'll say you are. Ugly old devil.

MARY

She is that.

SAM

Who's that with her?

MARY

Don't you know her? That's poor 'Tragedy'.
*The servants' bell rings. They all look up.*

## 83.  Mrs. Tranter's house. Garden room. Day.

MRS. TRANTER, MRS. POULTENEY, SARAH, ERNESTINA *and*
CHARLES, *sitting.*

MRS. TRANTER

Miss Woodruff, it is a pleasure to meet you. Are
you liking Lyme?

CHARLES *looks at* SARAH.

SARAH

Thank you ma'm. Yes.

MRS. TRANTER

Were you born far from Lyme?

SARAH

In Dorchester ma'm. It is not very far.
*A knock on the door.* MARY *and the* UNDERMAID
*enter with the tea.*

MRS. TRANTER

Ah, tea! Thank you Mary.
MRS. POULTENEY *glares at* MARY. MARY *ignores her.*
*The maids set the tea.*

MRS. POULTENEY (*to* ERNESTINA)

How long will you remain in Lyme, Miss
Freeman?

ERNESTINA

Oh, for the summer. I must say, Mrs. Poulteney, you look exceedingly well.

MRS. POULTENEY

At my age, Miss Freeman, spiritual health is all that counts.

ERNESTINA

Then I have no fears for you.

MRS. POULTENEY

With gross disorders on the streets it becomes ever more necessary to protect the sacredness of one's beliefs.

CHARLES

Gross disorders on the streets, Mrs. Poulteney?

MRS. POULTENEY

Certainly, Mr. Smithson. Even a disciple of Darwin, such as I understand you to be, could not fail to notice the rise of the animal about us. It no doubt pleases you, since it would accord with your view that we are all monkeys.

CHARLES

I must look more closely into it, Mrs. Poulteney, the next time I find myself on a street.

MARY *and the* UNDERMAID *leave the room.* MRS. TRANTER *begins to pour tea.*
*She passes a cup to* ERNESTINA.

SARAH (*to* MRS. TRANTER)

Please allow me to help you, Mrs. Tranter.

MRS. TRANTER

Thank you.

ERNESTINA *gives cup to* MRS. POULTENEY. SARAH *gives cup to* CHARLES.

MRS. POULTENEY

Your maid, for example. I have been informed that she was seen only this morning talking with a person. A young person.

CHARLES

Then it was no doubt Sam. My servant.

ERNESTINA *gives plate and napkin to* MRS. POULTENEY. SARAH *gives plate and napkin to* CHARLES.

*Her hand opens the napkin slightly. He looks down.*
*Inside the napkin is the corner of an envelope.*

## 84. Close up. Charles.
*He looks up quickly.*

## 85. Interior. The room.
ERNESTINA
Yes, I must say, Charles, your servant spends an
inordinate amount of his time talking to Mary.
CHARLES
What is the harm in that?
ERNESTINA
There is a world of difference between what may be
accepted in London and what is proper here.
CHARLES
But I do not understand what crime Mary and Sam,
by talking, appear to commit.
MRS. POULTENEY
Your future wife is a better judge than you are of
these things, Mr. Smithson. I know the girl in
question, I had to dismiss her. If you were older you
would know that one cannot be too strict in such
matters.
CHARLES
I bow to your far greater experience, madam.

## 86. The room
*They all sip tea in silence.*

## 87. Exterior. Mrs. Tranter's house. Day.
MRS. POULTENEY *and* SARAH *sitting in their carriage.*
ERNESTINA *and* MRS. TRANTER *stand by the carriage.* MRS.
POULTENEY *turns to* ERNESTINA.
MRS. POULTENEY
I am glad that you and I are of a mind, Miss
Freeman.
*The carriage drives out of the gate.* ERNESTINA *runs*
*towards the house.*

35

**88.** **Interior. Garden room.**

CHARLES, *alone, tearing open envelope. He takes out a
letter.*

**89.** **The letter**

'*I pray you to meet me at nine tonight. St. Michael's
Churchyard.*'

**90.** **Interior. Garden room.**

CHARLES *thrusts the envelope and letter into his pocket as*
ERNESTINA *rushes in, slamming the door, bursting into
tears. He takes her in his arms.*

CHARLES

My dearest. What is it?

ERNESTINA

Oh Charles, she's a horrid old woman, and I took
her part against you! How could I? I'm as horrid as
she is.

CHARLES

You're sweet and silly. Aren't you?

ERNESTINA

Yes.

CHARLES

What if this wicked maid and my rascal Sam should
fall in love? Are we to throw stones?

ERNESTINA

Only at Mrs. Poulteney!

*He laughs, kisses her eyes. She looks up at him, clings
to him.*

Eighty eight days to our wedding. It's an eternity.

CHARLES

Let us elope – and go to Paris.

ERNESTINA

Oh Charles – what wickedness!

*He kisses her lips quickly.*

CHARLES

If only the worthy Mrs. Poulteney could see us
now!

*She nuzzles into his chest, giggling.*

36

**91.   Close up. Charles. His face tense.**

**92.   Exterior. Churchyard. Night.**
SARAH *standing in the shadow of a large tombstone.*
*Footsteps approaching on gravel.*
CHARLES *approaching. He looks about.*
*Sound of organ suddenly from inside the church. (It con-*
*tinues in background throughout the scene.)* CHARLES *stops*
*still.*
SARAH'S *voice; a swift whisper:*
>                                 SARAH
Come here!
>        CHARLES *turns, goes to her.*
Thank you for coming. Thank you.
>        *They both speak in low voices.*
>                                CHARLES
How did you dare to behave in so impertinent and
presumptuous a manner? How dare you do such a
thing in front of Miss Freeman?
>                                 SARAH
I had no-one else to turn to.
>                                CHARLES
It must be obvious that it would be most improper
of me to interest myself further in your circum-
stances.
>                                 SARAH
Yes. It is obvious.
>        *She turns her face away. It is caught in moonlight.*
>                                CHARLES
Why do you not go to London? And find a new life?
>                                 SARAH
If I went to London I know what I should become. I
should become what some already call me in Lyme.
>                                CHARLES
My dear Miss Woodruff . . .
>                                 SARAH
I am weak. How should I not know it? I have
sinned.
>        *He stares at her.*

37

You cannot imagine . . . my suffering. My only happiness is when I sleep. When I wake, the nightmare begins.

*Footsteps. They freeze.*

## 93. The churchyard.

*The* VICAR *walking towards the church.*

## 94. The tombstone.

*She takes his hand, leads him to a darker place by a larger tombstone.*

*The organ grows louder. The church door closes. The organ dims.*

*They stand in the shadow of the tombstone.*

CHARLES

This is highly –

SARAH

Why am I born what I am? Why am I not born Miss Freeman?

CHARLES

That question were better not asked.

SARAH

I did not mean –

CHARLES

Envy is understandable in your –

SARAH

Not envy. Incomprehension.

*She looks at him.*

You must help me.

CHARLES

It is not in my power – to help you.

SARAH

I do not – I will not believe that.

CHARLES

What in heaven's name do you want of me?

SARAH

I want to tell you of what happened to me eighteen months ago.

*The organ suddenly stops.*

I beg you. You are my only hope. I shall be on the Undercliff tomorrow afternoon and the next afternoon. I shall wait for you.

CHARLES

I must go.
*He walks away.*

SARAH

I shall wait.

## 95. Interior. Hotel bedroom. Night. Present.

*MIKE and ANNA in bed. Moonlight. She is asleep. He is looking at her.*
*He quietly gets out of the bed, lights a cigarette, looks out of the window. He turns, looks back at the bed.*
*ANNA's foot is exposed. He moves to the bed, tucks the foot in, carefully. ANNA murmurs:*

ANNA

David . . .
*She wakes, looks up at him.*

MIKE

It's not David. It's Mike.

ANNA

What are you doing?

MIKE

Looking at you.

ANNA

Come back.
*He gets back into the bed. She puts her arm around him, and folds him to her breast.*

## 96. Interior. Dr. Grogan's study. Night.

*The room is bow-fronted and looks over the bay. A brass Georgian telescope rests on a table in the bow window.*
*GROGAN is pouring brandy. CHARLES is examining the telescope.*

GROGAN

Like my telescope?

CHARLES

It's most elegant, and indeed . . . most effective.

39

GROGAN

I use it to keep an eye out for mermaids. I'm delighted you dropped in. It's about time we met. Here. The best brandy in Lyme. I keep it for visitors from London, who share a taste for the good life.

CHARLES

Your good health, Doctor.

GROGAN

Yours. I understand you're a scientist, a seeker after fossils. Care for a cheroot?

CHARLES

Thank you. Yes, my interest is fossils. (*He smiles.*) I gather it is not yours.

GROGAN

When we know more of the living it will be time to pursue the dead.

*They sit back with their brandy and cheroots.*

CHARLES

Yes. I was introduced the other day to a specimen of the local flora that rather inclines me to agree with you. A very strange case, as far as I understand it. Her name is Woodruff.

GROGAN

Ah, yes. Poor 'Tragedy'. I'll tell you something. We know more about the fossils out there on the beach than we do about that girl's mind. There is a German doctor called Hartmann who has recently divided melancholia into several types. One he calls natural. By which he means one is born with a sad temperament. Another he calls occasional, by which he means springing from an occasion. The third class he calls obscure melancholia. By which he really means, poor man, that he doesn't know what the devil it is that caused it.

CHARLES

But she had an occasion, did she not?

GROGAN

Oh, come now, is she the first young woman to be jilted? No, no, she belongs to the third class – obscure melancholia. Listen to me – I'll tell you – in the strictest confidence – I was called in to see her – a ten-month ago. She was working as a seamstress, living alone, well, hardly living. Weeping without reason, unable to sleep, unable to talk. Melancholia as plain as the pox. I could see there was only one cure. To get her away from this place. But no, she wouldn't have it. What does she do? She goes to a house she knows is a living misery, to a mistress who doesn't know the difference between a servant and slave. And she won't be moved.

CHARLES

It's incomprehensible.

GROGAN

Not at all. Hartmann has an interesting thing to say about one of his patients. 'It was as if her torture had become her delight.'

CHARLES *throws the stub of his cheroot into the fire.*

CHARLES

And she has confided the real state of her mind to no-one?

GROGAN

She has not.

CHARLES

But if she did . . . if she could bring herself . . . to speak?

GROGAN

She would be cured. But she does not want to be cured.


## 97.   Exterior. Beach. Day. Present.

ANNA *barefoot in beach suit wanders along the shore picking up pebbles. She joins* MIKE *who lies on the beach, eyes closed. She stands above him.*

MIKE

Have a nice walk?

ANNA

Wonderful.

*She stretches, looks up at the sky.*

41

## 98. Exterior. Undercliff. Day.

*A dell, high up, overlooking the sea.*

SARAH *and* CHARLES *emerge through trees into the dell. She sits. He sits. She looks out to sea.*

SARAH

I was working as a governess. At the Talbots. His name was Varguennes.

## 99. Exterior. Beach. Day. Present.

ANNA *turns over suddenly onto her stomach and looks towards the Undercliff.*

MIKE

What's the matter?

*She is silent. He rolls over to look at her face.*

What's the matter? You look sad.

ANNA *(softly)*

No.

MIKE

Why are you sad?

ANNA

I'm not.

*He lies under her, pulls her down gently, kisses her. Her eyes close, then open. She looks towards the Undercliff.*

## 100. The Undercliff. Anna's P.O.V.

## 101. Exterior. The Undercliff. Day.

*The dell.* SARAH *is sitting on a hummock.* CHARLES *is sitting on a flat-topped block of flint. She looks out to sea. Her face is in profile to him.*

SARAH

His name was Varguennes. He was brought to the house after the wreck of his ship. He had a dreadful wound. His flesh was torn from his hip to his knee. He was in great pain. Yet he never cried out. Not the smallest groan. I admired his courage. I looked after him. I did not know then that men can be both very brave and very false.

*Pause.*

He was handsome. No man had ever paid me the kind of attentions he did, as he . . . was recovering. He told me I was beautiful, that he could not understand why I was not married. Such things. He would . . . mock me, lightly.

*Pause.*

I took pleasure in it.

*Pause.*

When I would not let him kiss my hand he called me cruel. A day came when I thought myself cruel as well.

CHARLES

And you were no longer cruel?

SARAH

No.

CHARLES

I understand.

SARAH (*fiercely*)

You cannot, Mr. Smithson. Because you are not a woman. You are not a woman born to be a farmer's wife but educated to be something . . . better. You were not born a woman with a love of intelligence, beauty, learning, but whose position in the world forbids her to share this love with another. And you are not the daughter of a bankrupt. You have not spent your life in penury. You are not . . . condemned. You are not an outcast.

CHARLES

Social privilege does not necessarily bring happiness.

SARAH

It brings the possibility of happiness.

**102.   Exterior. Day. Beach. Present.**

MIKE *and* ANNA *lying side by side. Her eyes are closed. He is looking at her.*

*Over this, the voices of* SARAH *and* CHARLES*:*

SARAH (*voice over*)

Varguennes recovered. He asked me to go back with him to France. He offered me . . .

43

Marriage?

ANNA *opens her eyes and looks at* MIKE.

## 103.    Exterior. Undercliff. Day.

SARAH

Yes. He left for Weymouth. He said he would wait there one week and then sail for France. I said I would never follow him, that I could not. But . . . after he had gone . . . my loneliness was so deep, I felt I would drown in it.

*Pause.*

I followed him. I went to the Inn where he had taken a room. It was not . . . a respectable place. I knew that at once. They told me to go up to his room. They looked at me . . . and smiled. I insisted he be sent for. He seemed overjoyed to see me. He was all that a lover should be. I had not eaten that day. He took me . . . to a private sitting room, ordered food.

*Pause.*

But he had changed. He was full of smiles and caresses but I knew at once that he was insincere. I saw that I had been an amusement for him, nothing more. He was a liar. I saw all this within five minutes of our meeting.

*Pause.*

Yet I stayed. I ate the supper that was served. I drank the wine he pressed on me. It did not intoxicate me. I think it made me see more clearly. Is that possible?

CHARLES

No doubt.

*Pause.*

SARAH

Soon he no longer bothered to hide the real nature of his intentions towards me. Nor could I pretend surprise. My innocence was false from the moment I chose to stay. I could tell you that he overpowered me, that he drugged me. But it is not so.

*She looks at him directly.*
I gave myself to him.
*Silence.*
I did it . . . so that I should never be the same again, so that I should be seen for the outcast I am. I knew it was ordained that I could never marry an equal. So I married shame. It is my shame . . . that has kept me alive, my knowing that I am truly not like other women. I shall never like them have children, a husband, the pleasures of a home. Sometimes I pity them. I have a freedom they cannot understand. No insult, no blame, can touch me. I have set myself beyond the pale. I am nothing. I am hardly human any more. I am the French Lieutenant's Whore.
    CHARLES *stands, walks over to her, looks down at her. For a moment it seems that he will take her in his arms. He straightens.*

                    CHARLES
You must leave Lyme.
    *Suddenly voices, laughter, from below, ascending.* SARAH *stands. She beckons to him silently and moves to the trees. He follows.*
    *The laughter comes closer.*
    SARAH *and* CHARLES *hide behind thick ivy. They look through it down to an ashgrove.*

104.  **The ashgrove. Their P.O.V.**
    *A girl and a boy, coming up towards them. The boy has his arm round her waist. He turns her to him and kisses her. They fall to the grass. The girl lies back. The boy kisses her.*

105.  **Close up. Sarah smiling at Charles.**

106.  **Charles.**
    *He stares at her.*

107.  **Charles and Sarah.**
    *They are looking at each other. Her smile fades. Silence.*

CHARLES
Please go. We must never meet alone again.
*She turns away.*
*A shrill laugh from below.* CHARLES *turns to look.*

**108.  The ashgrove.**
*The girl running downhill. The boy chasing her. Their figures flash between trees; a laugh; a scream; silence.*
CHARLES
Go. I will wait.
*She moves past him, into the ashgrove.*

**109.  Charles.**
*He watches her walk downhill through trees.*

**110.  Exterior. The dairy.**
MRS. FAIRLEY *and the* DAIRYMAN *outside the dairy. He is pouring milk.* MRS. FAIRLEY *gasps and stares.*

**111.  The dairy field. Mrs. Fairley's P.O.V.**
SARAH *walking openly downhill towards Lyme.*

**112.  Close up. Sarah. Walking calmly.**

**113.  Interior. Hotel Room. Night. Present.**
MIKE *is lying on a sofa, staring at the ceiling. Jazz is playing from a transistor radio.*

**114.  Exterior. Mrs. Poulteney's house. Night.**
*The house is dark.*
*A figure can be seen sitting by a dimly lit window.*

**115.  Interior. Sarah's bedroom. Night.**
SARAH *is sitting by the window. Candlelight. She is drawing.*
*The camera closes in on her and reveals that she is crying softly, as she draws.*

46

116. **The drawing.**
> *It is a self portrait.*
> *A sudden knock on the door.* SARAH *looks up*
>> MRS. FAIRLEY (*off screen*)
> Miss Woodruff! Miss Woodruff! Mrs Poulteney
> wishes to see you!

117. **Exterior. Street outside White Lion Hotel. Night.**
> *A small ragged boy running along the street.*
> *He stops at the White Lion, looks in quickly, goes in.*

118. **Interior. Hotel. Charles' sitting room. Night.**
> CHARLES *is lying on the sofa in dressing gown, staring at the*
> *ceiling. (Same set-up as shot 113.)*
> *An envelope slides under the door.*
> *He looks at it, stands quickly, goes to door, opens it.*
> *No-one.*
> *He closes door, picks up envelope, opens it, takes out letter.*

119. **The letter.**
> *'The secret is out. Am at the barn on the Undercliff. Only*
> *you stand between me and oblivion.'*

120. **Charles slowly puts the letter in his pocket.**

121. **Exterior. Dr. Grogan's house. Night.**
> CHARLES *knocking at the door. His carriage stands by the*
> *kerb.*
> *Thunder.*
> HOUSEKEEPER *opens the door.*
>> HOUSEKEEPER
> Yes?
>> CHARLES
> Forgive me. I must speak to Dr. Grogan.
>> HOUSEKEEPER
> Dr. Grogan is not here.
>> CHARLES
> Not here?

HOUSEKEEPER
He is at the asylum. He was called to the asylum.
CHARLES
Thank you.

**122. Interior. Asylum. Hall and corridor. Night.**

*A long empty stone corridor.*
*Silence.*
*Distant thunder.*
*An echoing cry.*
*A heavy* MAN *carrying keys comes towards camera, unlocks a door to the reception hall of the asylum.*
CHARLES *is waiting.*

MAN
Dr. Grogan is busy. He says to wait. Follow me.
*He leads* CHARLES *down the stone corridor to a door.*
CHARLES *goes in.*
You wait there.

**123. Interior. Asylum. Small room. Night.**

*The room is bare. A table, two chairs.*
CHARLES *goes to the window, which is barred. He stares out at the rain.*
*He turns abruptly.*

**124. Door of room. His P.O.V.**

*Two female patients are at the open door, looking at him. One of them is smiling.*

**125. Close up of Charles.**

*He gasps with shock.*

**126. The room.**

*One of the women goes towards him. She speaks as if in fever. As she speaks, she touches his body. He recoils, tries to tear her hand away.*

WOMAN
Help me – help me – help me – help me – help me – help me –
*The* MAN *comes in, seizes her, hits her, drags her out.*
*Shouts along the corridor. A scream.*

48

## 127.  Interior. Corridor.

CHARLES *goes into the corridor.*
*The* WOMAN *is being dragged along, screaming.*
*Various other sounds can be heard: moans, abrupt laughs,*
*whimpers, sudden shouts.*
*At the far end of the corridor a line of patients shuffles across.*
*A man in a dark suit herds them.*
CHARLES *turns swiftly, goes back into the room, closes the*
*door.*

## 128.  Interior. Room.

CHARLES *stands.*
*Sudden sound of footsteps approaching. The door opens –*
GROGAN *comes in, wiping his hands on a towel.*

GROGAN

Smithson. Yes, I can guess what you've come
about. Sorry I wasn't at home. I've been called to
attend a breech birth. Well, the fact is we don't
know where she is.

CHARLES

I'm sorry, I . . . I don't understand what you're
saying.

GROGAN

You don't know what's happened?

CHARLES

No.

GROGAN

Then why are you here?

CHARLES

I need your advice.

GROGAN

I'm not sure I've any left to give.
Miss Woodruff has disappeared.
Mrs. Poulteney dismissed her. There's a search
party out. I have offered five pounds to the man
who brings her back, or finds her body.

CHARLES

She is alive. I have just received a note from her.

GROGAN *stares at him.*
*A scream from another room.*

49

GROGAN

I must attend to the mother. Go to my house and
wait for me.

### 129. Exterior. The Undercliff. Night.

SARAH *running up hill through the trees.*
*Thunder.*

### 130. Grogan's study. Night.

GROGAN *pouring two glasses of brandy.*

GROGAN

Tell me the facts.

CHARLES

She wants to see me.
*He looks into* GROGAN's *eyes.*

GROGAN

I see.
*He looks at his watch.*
I must call off the search party. You know where
she is?

CHARLES

Yes.

GROGAN

Mmn. Well, you can't go to her, can you?

CHARLES

I am in your hands.

GROGAN

You *are* engaged to be married?
CHARLES *looks at him.*

CHARLES

I am.

GROGAN *goes to a book shelf and takes down a copy of*
*'Origin of Species'. He puts his hand on it, as on a*
*bible.*

GROGAN

Nothing that has been said in this room tonight or
that remains to be said shall go beyond these walls.
Well, now, you ask for my advice.
*He paces up and down the room.*

I am a young woman of superior intelligence and some education. I am not in full command of my emotions. What is worse, I have fallen in love with being a victim of fate. Enter a young god. Intelligent. Goodlooking. Kind. I have but one weapon. The pity I inspire in him. So what do I do? I seize my chance. One day, when I am walking where I have been forbidden to walk, I show myself to someone I know will report my crime to the one person who will not condone it. I disappear, under the strong presumption that it is in order to throw myself off the nearest clifftop. And then – *in extremis*, I cry to my saviour for help.

CHARLES
What in God's name are you talking about?

GROGAN
I have spoken to Mrs. Poulteney's housekeeper. She was at the dairy on the Undercliff. The girl walked out of the woods under her nose. It was deliberate. She wanted to be seen. Presumably to compromise you.

CHARLES
But why should she wish to harm me?

GROGAN
Listen to me. I have known many prostitutes. I hasten to add – in pursuance of my own profession, not theirs. And I wish I had a guinea for every one I have heard gloat over the fact that a majority of their victims are husbands and fathers.

CHARLES
But she is not a prostitute! Neither is she a fiend!

GROGAN
My dear man, you are half in love with her.
CHARLES *stares at him.*

CHARLES
On my most sacred honour nothing improper has passed between us.

GROGAN

I believe you. But let me ask you this. Do you wish to hear her? Do you wish to see her? Do you wish to touch her?

CHARLES *sits, covers his face.*

CHARLES

Oh my dear Grogan, if you knew . . . the confusion . . . my life is in.

GROGAN

You are not the first person to doubt his choice of bride.

*Pause.*

I will go to see the lady. I shall tell her you have been called away. And you must go away, Smithson.

CHARLES

Yes.

*He looks at* GROGAN.

I shall honour my vows to Miss Freeman.

GROGAN

I know of a private asylum in Salisbury. Miss Woodruff . . . will be kindly treated . . . and helped. Would you bear the expense?

CHARLES (*slowly*)

Yes. I would bear the expense.


**131. Exterior. White Lion. Dawn.**

*The storm has cleared. The growing dawn is still, clear.*


**132. Interior. Charles' sitting room.**

CHARLES *stands by the window. He looks out at the sky. His expression is purposeful.*
*He turns, goes into his bedroom. Through the open door we see him dressing.*


**133. The Undercliff. Dawn.**

CHARLES *striding swiftly through the woods. The sun slants through the trees.*
*Dense birdsong.*
*He climbs until he sees the sea stretched out below.*

*He stops.*
*The thatched roof of a barn.*

## 134. Exterior. Barn.

CHARLES *approaches it. Silence.*
*He looks in at a small window, turns, looks about, opens*
*door, enters.*

## 135. Interior. Barn.

*Sunlight floods through the window.*
*He peers into the shadows, suddenly perceives a bonnet*
*hanging on a nail, by a partition.*
*He goes to partition, looks over.*

## 136. Sarah curled under her coat, asleep.

## 137. The barn.

CHARLES *withdraws to the door of the barn, stands a*
*moment, speaks.*

CHARLES

Miss Woodruff.
*A rustle from behind the partition.* SARAH *looks over,*
*sees him. Her hand goes to her mouth. She goes back.*
*He stands.*
*She comes out and walks towards him.*
*She stops a few feet away from him.*
Have you passed the night here?
*She nods.*
Are you cold?
*She shakes her head.*
Do not . . . fear. I have come to help you.
*He lays his hand on her shoulder.*
*She seizes his hand, raises it to her lips, kisses it.*
*He snatches his hand away.*
Pray control yourself, I –

SARAH

I cannot.
*She slips to her knees, cries softly.*
I cannot.

*He bends to her, slowly lifts her. She stands. His hands remain on her arms. She looks up at him. He takes her into his arms. She sways into his embrace. He kisses her deeply, crushing her body to him.*
*A giggle is heard, from outside the barn.*
CHARLES *breaks away from* SARAH, *looks at the door, goes to it, opens it.*

**138.   Exterior. Barn. Charles' P.O.V.**
SAM *and* MARY, *staring in astonishment.*

**139.   Exterior. The barn door. Their P.O.V.**
CHARLES *standing. Behind him* SARAH. *She disappears from view.*

**140.   Exterior. Barn.**
CHARLES *walks towards them.*
>                    CHARLES
> What are you doing here?
>                       SAM
> Out walking, Mr. Charles.
>                 CHARLES (*to* MARY)
> Kindly leave us a moment.
> MARY *bobs and walks away.*
>                 CHARLES (*to* SAM)
> I have come here to help this lady. At the request of the physician who is treating her. He is fully aware of the circumstances.
>                       SAM
> Yes, sir.
>                    CHARLES .
> Which must on no account be disclosed.
>                       SAM
> I understand.
>                    CHARLES
> Does she?
>                       SAM
> She won't say nothing. On my life.
> *They stare at each other.*

On my solemn oath, Mr. Charles.
*SAM goes to join MARY. CHARLES watches them walk away.*
*He turns and goes back into the barn.*

## 141. Exterior. The woods.

*SAM and MARY helpless in silent laughter.*

## 142. Interior. Barn.

*SARAH is standing. He goes to her.*
CHARLES
I have taken unpardonable advantage of your situation. I am wholly to blame.
*Pause.*
You must go to Exeter. There is talk in the town of commiting you to an institution. You need not take it seriously. But you will save yourself . . . embarrassment if you do not return to Lyme. Where are your belongings?
SARAH
At the coach depot.
CHARLES
I will have them sent to the depot in Exeter. Walk to Axmouth Cross. Wait for the coach there. Take the money in this purse.
*He gives her the purse.*
SARAH
Thank you.
*He gives her a card.*
CHARLES
Here is my lawyer's address. Let him know where you are. I will instruct him to send you more money.
SARAH
Thank you.
*They look at each other.*
I shall never see you again.
CHARLES
No.

*Pause.*

You are a remarkable person, Miss Woodruff.

SARAH

Yes, I am a remarkable person.


**143. Exterior. Undercliff. Day. Present.**

ANNA, *wearing jeans, weaves her way through the crowd towards* MIKE. MIKE *is in costume, eating salad. She sits beside him.*

*In the background a mobile canteen — the unit eating lunch at trestle tables: some playing football.* 'ERNESTINA' *and* 'MARY' *in costume at a table.*

ANNA

I'm going. To London.

MIKE

Yes.

*Pause.*

Do you have to?

ANNA

I don't have any more scenes to do in Lyme.

MIKE

Yes. Well, have a good time.

*She looks at him.*

ANNA

David's coming in from New York.

MIKE

How nice for you.

*He takes her hand.*

No, it will be nice for you. Nice for him, too.

ANNA

I'll miss you.

*The* THIRD ASSISTANT *approaches.*

MIKE

When do we go to London?

THIRD ASSISTANT (*to* MIKE)

Tuesday or Wednesday.

I'll drive you up to The Cups straight after lunch. Okay?

MIKE

Right.

56

THIRD ASSISTANT (*to* ANNA)

See you in Exeter, Anna. Think of us slogging away.

ANNA

I will.

THIRD ASSISTANT *goes.*

MIKE

I must see you in London.

ANNA

We'd have to be careful.

MIKE

I must see you.

ANNA

Yes. Yes.

*Voice on loud hailer: 'Right everybody. We're moving up to The Cups.'*


## 144.  Interior. The Cups. Sitting room.

SAM *folding shirts.* CHARLES *comes in.*

CHARLES

Sam, I want you to go to London today.
Open up the house. I'll be leaving myself tomorrow. Change of plan.

SAM

I see, sir. (*He clears his throat.*)
This doesn't have any bearing on your future plans, I . . . uuh . . . I trust, sir?

CHARLES

My future plans? What are you talking about?

SAM

Well . . . I've got to think about my future, sir.

CHARLES *glares at him.*

CHARLES

Have you? Well, your immediate future is to go to London today. Is that clear?

SAM

Yes, Mr. Charles.


## 145.  Interior. Mrs. Tranter's house. Hall. Day.

MARY *opening front door.* CHARLES.

CHARLES

Ah. Good afternoon.

MARY

Good afternoon, sir. Miss Ernestina is in the garden.

CHARLES

Thank you.

*He enters, takes off his hat and gloves and gives them to her. He clears his throat, speaks quietly.*

Sam . . . has explained the circumstances of this morning?

MARY

Yes, sir.

CHARLES

You . . . understand?

MARY

Yes, sir.

*He feels in his waistcoat pocket and brings out a golden coin. He presses it into her hand.*

MARY

Oh sir, I don't want that.

*He moves down the hall.*

*She looks at the coin.*


**146.  Interior. Garden room.**

CHARLES *walks through the room to the window. He looks out into the garden.*

ERNESTINA *is sitting with tea, reading a book.*

CHARLES *stands, heavy and pensive, looking out on the scene.*

*He walks into the garden.*


**147.  Exterior. Mrs. Tranter's house. Garden. Day.**

CHARLES *strides across the lawn.*

CHARLES

Good afternoon!

ERNESTINA

Charles!

*He takes her hand.*

58

So you have actually deigned to desert the world of the fossil for me. I am honoured.

CHARLES

I assure you, the true charm of the world resides in this garden.

ERNESTINA

Honeyed words.

*She squeezes his hand.*

CHARLES

My dearest, I am afraid I must leave you for a few days. I must go to London.

ERNESTINA

To London?

CHARLES

To see Montague – my lawyer.

ERNESTINA

Oh Charles!

CHARLES

It's unavoidable, I'm afraid. Apparently there are matters outstanding – to do with the marriage settlement. Your father is a most scrupulous person.

ERNESTINA

What does he want?

CHARLES

Justice for you.

ERNESTINA

Sweet justice, that takes you away from me.

CHARLES

Ernestina, I know our private affections are the paramount consideration, but there is also a legal and contractual side to matrimony which is –

ERNESTINA

Fiddlesticks!

CHARLES

My dearest Tina –

ERNESTINA

I am weary of Lyme. I see you so little.

CHARLES

I shall be back in three days.

ERNESTINA

Kiss me then. To seal your promise.

*He hesitates for a second, then kisses her.*


148. **Exterior. Endicott's Hotel. Exeter. Evening.**

SARAH *walks slowly up the hill from the railway station.*

*She carries two suitcases.*

*She stops for a rest.*

*She sees Endicott's Hotel.*


149. **Interior. Real tennis court. Lords. London. Day.**

*(N.B. Real tennis is the old English game of tennis, played in an indoor court.)*

CHARLES *and* MONTAGUE *in the middle of a rally.*

*The rally is violent, intense.* CHARLES *hits the ball savagely and wins the point.*


150. **Interior. Dressing room. Lords. Day.**

MONTAGUE *dressing.* CHARLES *comes in, dressed.*

MONTAGUE

Goodness, Charles, you were in cracking form. Sharp as a razor. What's the answer? Country grub?

CHARLES *laughs shortly.*

CHARLES

It's good to . . . hit a ball.

MONTAGUE

You were hitting it as though you hated it.

CHARLES *closes the door.*

CHARLES

Harry . . . a word . . . you will be hearing from a person. A Miss Woodruff – from Exeter. She will give you her address. I'd like you to send her some money for me.

MONTAGUE

Of course. How much?

CHARLES

Fifty pounds.

MONTAGUE

Of course.
*Pause.*
Miss Woodruff.

CHARLES

Yes.
*Pause.*
And I want to hear . . . nothing more about it.
MONTAGUE *looks at him.*

MONTAGUE

You shan't.

151. **Interior. Hotel room. Exeter. Evening.**
SARAH *is alone in the room.*
*She is taking parcels from a canvas bag.*
*She unwraps the first and takes from it a nightgown.*
*She lays it on the bed.*
*She unwraps the second parcel. It is a dark green merino
shawl. She holds it, feels it, brings it to touch her cheek. She
shakes the shawl out and then arranges it round the shoulders
of the laid-out nightgown.*
*She studies the image for a moment, goes through the open
door into her small sitting room, where a fire burns, and puts
a kettle on the hearth.*

152. **Exterior. Charles' Kensington house. Evening.**
*Lamplight.*
*A carriage draws up.* CHARLES *jumps out, walks quickly up
the steps to his house and knocks on the door.*
*He waits.*
*He knocks again, violently.*

153. **Interior. Kensington house. Hall. Evening.**
SAM *walking towards front door.*
*He opens it.* CHARLES *strides in.*

CHARLES

Where the devil have you been?

SAM

I'm sorry sir.

61

CHARLES

Are you deaf?

CHARLES *walks up the stairs.*

Lay out my clothes. I'm dining at my club.

SAM

Yes, sir. Can I have one word with you, sir?

CHARLES

No. You can't.


## 154. Interior. London club. Evening.

CHARLES *enters the smoking room*
*Two men of* CHARLES' *age,* NATHANIEL DYSON *and* SIR
TOM BURGH, *drinking at a table.*

SIR TOM

Charley! What the devil are you doing out of the
matrimonial lock-up?

CHARLES

Good evening, Tom. Nathaniel, how are you?

NAT *raises a languid hand.*

On parole, you know. The dear girl's down in
Dorset taking the waters.

SIR TOM

I hear she's the rose of the season. Nat says:
'Damned Charley. Best girl and best match.' Ain't
fair, is it, Nat?

CHARLES

Would you discuss a punch and bubbly?

SIR TOM

We would certainly discuss a punch and bubbly.
James! Punch and bubbly!

CHARLES *sits.*

How goes the hunting in Dorset, Charles? And
how go you for hounds? I can offer you a brace of
the best Northumberland. Real angels. Do you
know who their granpapa was? Tornado. You
recall Tornado – at Cambridge?

CHARLES

I recall him. So do my ankles.

*Servants bring a bowl of punch and champagne.*

62

SIR TOM

Aye, he took a fancy to you. Always bit what he loved.

*Servants pour champagne.*

What a profoundly good idea this was, Charley.

*He raises his glass.*

Dear old Tornado – God rest his soul.

CHARLES *and* NAT *raise their glasses, and murmur:* 'God rest his soul'.


## 155. Interior. Club. Dining room.

*The three men at a table.*

*Waiter approaching the table with two decanters of port.*

*He places them.*

SIR TOM

Bravo! Port is essential to wash down the claret.

NAT

As claret was essential to wash down the punch.

SIR TOM

As punch was essential to sluice the champagne.

*They are all drunk,* CHARLES *the most drunk.*

NAT

What follows?

SIR TOM

What follows? A little drive round town follows. That most essentially follows.

*He pours more port for them all.*

CHARLES

Tom, dear old fellow, you're a damn good fellow.

SIR TOM

So are you, my Charley boy. We're all damn good fellows.

SIR TOM *stands.*

On we go gentlemen.

NAT *stands.*

*The dining room is empty.*

CHARLES

Where are we going?

Where damn good fellows always go of a jolly
night. Eh, Tom? To Kate Hamilton's. Bless her
heart.

SIR TOM

The Bishop's son has hit it, Charley.
(*He puts a finger to his lips.*). But not a word to his old
man.

CHARLES *stands and collapses. They catch him, and
hold him up between them.*

*The group staggers across the room and crashes into a
table, knocking it over. They ricochet into another
table.*

*With cries from* SIR TOM *and* NAT *of 'Whoops!'
'Steady there!' and finally 'Charge!' the group crashes
into table after table along the length of the dining
room.*

*Three expressionless waiters watch them.*

*They all collapse in a heap on the floor.* CHARLES'
*eyes closed.*

SIR TOM

I don't think our dear Charley is going anywhere
tonight, old boy, do you?


## 156.   Exterior. Charles' Kensington house. Morning.

*A* MESSENGER *walking along the street. He goes up the
steps of* CHARLES' *house, knocks at door.* SAM *opens it.*
MESSENGER *hands* SAM *an envelope.*

MESSENGER

For Mr. Smithson from Mr. Montague.

SAM

Thank you very much.
*He shuts the door.*


## 157.   Interior. Charles' Kensington house. Hall. Morning.

SAM *is looking at the envelope.*

**158.** **Interior. Kensington house. Kitchen. Morning.**

SAM *steaming open the envelope. He takes out a letter. He reads it. He replaces it, picks up some gum, begins to seal the envelope.*

**159.** **Interior. Kensington house. Study. Morning.**

CHARLES *lying, half dressed, asleep, on a Chesterfield.* SAM *enters, goes to* CHARLES, *bends over him.*

SAM

Mr. Charles . . . Mr. Charles . . .

CHARLES *opens his eyes.*

A letter's just come for you, sir.

Special messenger, from Mr. Montague.

*He gives the letter to* CHARLES.

CHARLES *looks at the handwriting on the envelope.*

**160.** **The envelope.**

*In* SARAH'*s handwriting: For the Personal Attention of Mr. Charles Smithson.*

*His hands tear open the envelope. He opens the letter.*

*The letter: 'Endicott's Family Hotel, Exeter'.*

**161.** **Interior. Kensington house. The study. Morning.**

CHARLES *looks up from the letter to* SAM.

CHARLES

Bring me tea.

**162.** **Interior. Kensington house. The study. Morning.**

*Later.*

CHARLES *at desk, in dressing gown, writing a letter.*

SAM *comes in, places tray of tea on side table, remains standing.* CHARLES *continues to write.*

**163.** **The writing paper. Charles' hand.**

*'There can be no question of further communication between us – '*

CHARLES' *hand stops writing.*

**164.** **Charles and Sam.**

CHARLES *turns to* SAM.

CHARLES

What is it?

SAM

I would like your advice, sir.

CHARLES

On what subject?

SAM

My ambition is to go into business, sir – in due
course.

CHARLES *turns back to his letter and continues to write.*

CHARLES

Business?

SAM

Yes, sir.

CHARLES

What sort of business?

SAM

Drapers and haberdashers. I've set my heart on a
little shop.

CHARLES

Would that not be a somewhat expensive under-
taking?

SAM

It would cost two hundred and eighty pounds.

CHARLES

And how much have you put by?

SAM

Thirty pounds. Over the last five years. So I was
wondering if you could help me.

CHARLES *turns to look at him, as he picks up the letter
from his desk, calmly tears it into pieces and puts the
pieces into the pocket of his gown.*

CHARLES

I can't say it sounds a very practical idea to me,
Sam.

SAM *stares at him coldly.*

SAM

I am very enthusiastic about the idea myself, sir.
Very.

CHARLES

I see. Well, let me think about it. I shall certainly be happy to think about it.

Pack, will you? We're going to Lyme today.

SAM

To Lyme, sir?

CHARLES

To Lyme. Yes.


**165.  Interior. Bar in London. Present.**

ANNA *and* MIKE *at table with drinks.*

ANNA

How are you. How's it going?

MIKE

All right. Bloody hard. I'm exhausted. I've been dying for you.

ANNA

Mmmn.

MIKE

How's it been? Have you been having a good time?

ANNA

I don't know . . . it's all so unreal . . .

MIKE

What do you mean?

ANNA

The world isn't real . . . up here.

MIKE

What about your boy friend? Isn't he real?

ANNA

I miss Sarah. I can't wait to get back. I can't wait to be in Exeter.

MIKE

You know what's going to happen in Exeter? I'm going to have you in Exeter.

ANNA

Are you now?

MIKE

Yes. (*He smiles.*) I am.

**166.  Train arriving at station. Afternoon.**
*Large signs:* EXETER.
*The train stops.* SAM *runs along platform to meet* CHARLES,
*who descends from a first-class compartment.*

SAM

Carriage to Lyme, sir?
CHARLES *looks up at the sky.*

CHARLES

It's going to rain – badly.
*They both look up.*
We had better stay the night. We'll put up at The
Ship.

SAM

But we're expected in Lyme, sir.

CHARLES

We'll be there in the morning. I think I'll stretch my
legs. You go on with the baggage.

SAM

Shall I order dinner, sir?

CHARLES

I'll decide when I come in. I may attend Evensong
at the Cathedral.
CHARLES *walks down the platform.*


**167.  Exterior. Back street. Exeter. Dusk.**
CHARLES *appears in the street. He looks about him. A small
boy passes.* CHARLES *stops him, asks him a question.
The boy leads* CHARLES *to a corner and points.*
CHARLES *gives him a coin and disappears round the corner.*


**168.  Exterior. Endicott's Family Hotel.**
CHARLES *approaching. He enters.*


**169.  Interior. Hotel. The hall.**
CHARLES *in the hall. The door of a room is ajar. He knocks
and goes in.* MRS. ENDICOTT *rises.*

MRS. ENDICOTT

A room, sir?

68

CHARLES

No, I . . . that is, I wish to speak to one of your . . . a Miss Woodruff?

MRS. ENDICOTT

Oh the poor young lady, sir, she was a-coming downstairs yesterday morning and she slipped, sir. She's turned her ankle terrible. I wanted to ask the doctor, sir, but she won't hear of it.

CHARLES

I have to see her . . . on a business matter.

MRS. ENDICOTT

Ah. A gentleman of the law?

CHARLES

Yes.

MRS. ENDICOTT

Then you must go up, sir. (*Shouting.*) Betty Anne!

*The maid,* BETTY ANNE, *appears.*

Take this gentleman to Miss Woodruff's room.

## 170. Interior. Landing.

BETTY ANNE *leads* CHARLES *to a door. She knocks and opens it.*

BETTY ANNE

A gentleman to see you, Miss.

CHARLES *steps into the room.* BETTY ANNE *closes the door behind him.*

## 171. Interior. Sarah's sitting room.

SARAH *is sitting in a chair by the fire, her naked feet on a stool. One ankle is bandaged. A blanket over her knees. She is wearing her green shawl over a long sleeved nightgown. Her hair is loose.*

*She looks up at him, swiftly, then down.*

CHARLES

I was passing through Exeter.

*Pause.*

Had I not better go at once and fetch a doctor?

SARAH

He would only advise me to do what I am already doing.

CHARLES

You are not in pain?
*She shakes her head.*
At any rate be thankful that it did not happen on the
Undercliff.

SARAH

Yes.
*Silence.*
Do sit down.
> CHARLES *sits by the table. He looks at her. The
> firelight flickers over her white nightgown, her face,
> her hair.*
> *Rain patters on the window.*
> SARAH *raises her hands suddenly to her mouth, bends
> her head, begins to cry quietly.*

CHARLES

Miss Woodruff . . . please . . . I should not have
come . . . I meant not to . . .
> *She shakes her head violently. She stops crying, looks
> at him.*

SARAH

I thought never to see you again.
> *She looks down. He closes his eyes.*
> *Silence.*
> *Suddenly a cascade of coal falls from the fire. One or
> two bounce out of the grate and onto the edge of
> SARAH's blanket. She jerks the blanket away.*
> CHARLES *stands quickly and shovels the coals back into
> the fire. He snatches the blanket, which is smoulder-
> ing, throws it on the floor and stamps on it. He picks it
> up, slaps it and then carefully places it across her legs,
> bending over her. As he is doing so, her hand rests on
> his.*
> *They look at each other. Their fingers interlace.*
> *He drops to his knees. They kiss violently. He half
> withdraws. She presses him back to her mouth. They
> kiss again. He raises her head and looks at her. They
> kiss again. The chair rolls back. He turns to look at the
> bedroom door, which is open.*

70

*He stands, pulls her up. She falls towards him. He picks her up in his arms. The shawl falls. He kisses her mouth and her breasts as she lies back in his arms. He carries her into the bedroom.*
*In the dim light of the bedroom he throws her across the bed. She lies, one arm flung back.*
*Sound of stripping of clothes. He appears, goes to the bed. His body covers her. He moves upon her.*
*He enters her. She cries out with pain. He stops. She draws him to her. He makes love to her.*

CHARLES

Oh, my dearest . . . my sweetest angel . . . my sweetest angel . . . oh, Sarah.
*Gasps. A long groan.*
*They are still.*

## 172. Exterior. Endicott's Hotel. Evening.

SAM *looking at hotel. He goes in the door. Camera pans to see through window* SAM *talking to* BETTY ANNE. *He gives her a coin.*

## 173. Interior. Sarah's bedroom. Evening.

SARAH *and* CHARLES *on the bed. They lie in silence. Her hand touches and caresses his. He looks at her.*

CHARLES

I was . . . the first.

SARAH

Yes.

CHARLES

Why did you lie to me – about the Frenchman?

SARAH

I don't know.

CHARLES

Does he exist?

SARAH

Oh, yes. He exists. I did follow him to Weymouth, to the Inn. As I drew near I saw him come out, with a woman. The kind of woman one cannot mistake. When they had gone, I walked away.

CHARLES
But then – why did you tell me – ?
SARAH
I don't know. I cannot explain.
*She puts a finger on his mouth.*
Not now.
CHARLES
I must make myself free.
SARAH
I ask nothing of you.
CHARLES
I am to blame. I knew when I came here –
SARAH
I wished it so. I wished it so.
*He strokes her hair.*
CHARLES
Sarah – it is the sweetest name.
SARAH
I have long imagined a day such as this. I have
longed . . . for it. I was lost from the moment I saw
you.
CHARLES
I . . . too.
*Pause.*
I must go to Lyme, to see her, to tell her. You must
give me a day's grace. You will wait for me? Won't
you? I shall come back for you, my sweet . . .
mystery.
*He takes her in his arms, kisses her.*

**174.  Exterior. Endicott's Hotel. Evening.**
SAM *standing at a doorway, looking up at a dimly lit
window.*

**175.  Interior. Sarah's sitting room. Evening.**
CHARLES *has dressed. They stand at the door of the room.
She smiles. He kisses her. She holds him.*

72

SARAH

Do what you will. Or what you must. Now I know there was truly a day upon which you loved me, I can bear anything. You have given me . . . the strength to live.

**176. Exterior. Exeter Station. Platform. Night. Present.**

*The London train is standing at the platform.* MIKE *runs up the platform with a sandwich to the open window of a carriage.* ANNA *is at the window looking out. Porters banging doors. He gives her the sandwich.*

MIKE

Cheese and onion.

ANNA

Perfect.

*She bites into sandwich.*

MIKE

I'm losing you.

ANNA

What do you mean?

MIKE

I'm losing you.

ANNA

What are you talking about? I'm just going to London for –

MIKE

Stay tonight.

ANNA

I can't.

MIKE

Why not? You're a free woman.

ANNA

Yes. I am.

MIKE

I'm going mad.

ANNA

No you're not.

*She leans through the window and kisses him.*

MIKE (*intensely*)

I want you so much.

ANNA (*with mock gravity*)
But you've just had me. In Exeter.
*She bursts into laughter. He grins slowly. A woman
looks up at them.
The train moves out of the station. She remains at the
window. He remains on the platform.*

## 177. Close up. Ernestina.
*She is listening. Sound of front door closing, of* MARY's *and*
CHARLES' *voices. Her face lights up.
Sound of quick knock on her door and it opening.*

ERNESTINA
Charles!
*Sound of door closing. Silence. She frowns.*
What is it? Charles? What is it?

## 178. Ernestina's sitting room. Day.
CHARLES *stands by the door.*

CHARLES
Please sit down.
*She does so, slowly.*

ERNESTINA
What has happened?
Why do you look at me like that?

CHARLES
I do not know how to begin to say what I must. I
have come to tell you the truth.

ERNESTINA
The truth? What truth?

CHARLES
That I have, after many hours of the deepest, the
most painful consideration, come to the conclusion
that I am not worthy of you.

ERNESTINA
Not *worthy* of me?

CHARLES
Totally unworthy.
*She laughs.*

ERNESTINA
You are joking.

74

CHARLES

No.

*Pause.*

ERNESTINA

Will you kindly explain to me what you are saying?

CHARLES

The terms your father offered in the settlement were more than generous –

ERNESTINA

But you despise the idea of marrying into trade.

CHARLES

I do not despise it – I –

ERNESTINA

Then what are you saying?

*Pause.*

CHARLES

Ernestina, I have realised, in these last days, that too great a part of my regard for you has always been ignoble. I was far more tempted by your father's fortune than I have cared to admit. Now I have seen that to be the truth –

ERNESTINA

Are you saying you have never loved me?

CHARLES

I am not worthy of you.

ERNESTINA

Charles . . . I know I am spoiled. I know I am not . . . unusual. But under your love and protection . . . I believed I should become better. I would do anything . . . you see . . . I would abandon anything . . . to make you happy . . .

*She covers her face.*

*He stands still.*

*She suddenly looks at him.*

ERNESTINA

You are lying. Something else has happened.

*Pause.*

CHARLES

Yes.

75

ERNESTINA

Who?

CHARLES

You do not know her.

ERNESTINA *(dully)*

I don't know her?

CHARLES

I have known her . . . many years. I thought the attachment was broken. I discovered in London . . . that it is not.

*Pause.*

ERNESTINA

Why did you not tell me this at the beginning?

CHARLES

I hoped to spare you the pain of it.

ERNESTINA

Or yourself the shame of it. Who is she? What woman could be so vile as to make a man break his vows? I can guess. She is married.

CHARLES

I will not discuss her. I came to tell you the truth, the most terrible decision of my life –

ERNESTINA

The truth! You are a liar. My father will drag your name – both your names, through the mire. You will be spurned and detested by all who know you. You will be hounded out of England, you will be –

ERNESTINA *sways, slumps to the floor.*

## 179. Interior. Endicott's Hotel. Bedroom window. Day.

SARAH *sitting on the bed, which is made. She covers her face, begins to cry. She stands, goes to the window, looks out.*

## 180. Exterior. Exeter Station. Her P.O.V.

*A goods train going out.*

## 181. Interior. Bedroom window.

SARAH *at the window, crying.*

**182. Interior. Charles' hotel room. Lyme. Day.**

CHARLES *comes in and slams the door.*
*He opens the window and takes in a long breath of air.*
*He goes to writing table and nervously sets out writing materials. He begins to write 'Dear Mr. Freeman – '*
*A sharp knock on the door.* SAM *enters with brandy.*

CHARLES

What the devil do you want? I didn't ring.

SAM

I brought you a glass of brandy, sir. I thought you might want it.

CHARLES *takes brandy and sips.*

It's never true, sir.

CHARLES *looks at him.*

CHARLES

Yes, it is true. Miss Freeman and I are no longer to marry. Now go. And keep your mouth shut.

*He bends to the paper.* SAM *does not move.* CHARLES *looks up.*

Did you hear what I said?

SAM

Yes, sir. Only, with respect, I have to consider my own situation.

CHARLES

What?

SAM

Will you be residing in London from now on, sir?

CHARLES

We shall probably go abroad.

SAM

Ah. Well, I beg to advise you that I won't be accompanying you. And I'm not coming back to Exeter either. I'm leaving your employ. As I ought to have done weeks ago, when all this started.

CHARLES *stands.*

CHARLES

Go to hell!

*They glare at each other.* SAM *opens the door. He turns.*

77

SAM

I don't fancy nowhere, *sir*, as I might meet a friend of yours.

> SAM *goes out slamming the door.* CHARLES *rips it open.*

CHARLES

Sam!

SAM

If you wish for attention, ring for one of the hotel domestics.

> *He goes down the stairs.* CHARLES *slams the door and stands.*
> *He picks up the brandy glass and hurls it into the fireplace.*

## 183.  Interior. Sarah's sitting room. Exeter. Day.

> SARAH *is dressing. She puts the shawl around her shoulders and looks at herself in the mirror. She hears sounds of children in the street, goes to the window and looks down at them.*
> *She turns back into the room, picks up a kerchief which* CHARLES *has left behind him. She fondles it, puts it down.*

## 184.  Interior. Hotel. Lyme. Landing. Day.

CHARLES

Mr. Barnes! Make up my bill! I'm leaving.

VOICE

Rightaway, Mr. Smithson.

> CHARLES *goes back into his room and slams the door.*

## 185.  Interior. Hotel room.

> *The room is in chaos. Wardrobe doors and cupboard drawers wide open, clothes spilling out.* CHARLES *is trying to pack his belongings into two large trunks. He flings the clothes in. A quick knock at the door.* GROGAN *comes in.* CHARLES *looks at him, continues packing, moving from wardrobe to trunk.*

GROGAN

I await your explanation, my friend.

CHARLES

I am leaving Lyme.

*He pulls at a drawer in a chest of drawers. The drawer comes out and falls with a crash.*

Damn!

GROGAN

I have come from Miss Freeman. I have put her to sleep. When she wakes you could be by her. It is not too late – to mend the matter.

CHARLES

It is far too late.

GROGAN *watches him.*

GROGAN

I have been told by Mrs. Tranter that there is another woman.

CHARLES

I must ask you not to reveal her name.

GROGAN

You ask me to follow your example in deceit?

CHARLES

I believed the deceit to be necessary.

GROGAN

As you believed the satisfaction of your lust to be necessary.

CHARLES

I will not accept that word.

GROGAN

You had better learn to. It is the one the world will use.

CHARLES

Let it do so.

*He continues to pack.*

GROGAN

You will marry the lady?

CHARLES

That is my deepest wish.

GROGAN

You have committed a crime. It will fester in you all your life.

CHARLES *stops packing and looks at him.*

CHARLES

No . . . Grogan. You do not understand. She is remarkable. She is free. I am free also. She has given me this freedom. I shall embrace it.
*Silence.*

GROGAN

So be it.

## 186. Exterior. Endicott's Hotel. Exeter. Night.

*A carriage comes down the street and draws up.* CHARLES *gets out and goes into the hotel.*

## 187. Interior. Endicott's Hotel. Exeter. Hall. Night.

CHARLES *comes in the front door.* MRS. ENDICOTT *looks out of her room.* CHARLES *gives her a coin.*

CHARLES

Miss Woodruff expects me. I'll find my own way.
*He turns to the stairs.*

MRS. ENDICOTT

The young lady's left, sir.

CHARLES

Left? You mean gone out?

MRS. ENDICOTT

No, sir. I mean left.
*He stares at her.*
She took the London train this afternoon.

CHARLES

What?

MRS. ENDICOTT

She took the three o'clock to London. Didn't leave no address.

CHARLES

You're a liar.
*He turns and bounds up the stairs.*
Sarah!

MRS. ENDICOTT

Where are you going?

## 188. Interior. Sarah's room.

CHARLES *bursts in.*

80

MRS. ENDICOTT (*off screen*)

What are you doing? You can't do that.

CHARLES *goes to the writing table, shelves, etc., lifts objects, table cloth, goes into bedroom through open door.*

MRS. ENDICOTT *comes into the room.*

MRS. ENDICOTT

You've no right! You're trespassing.

CHARLES *stares at the unmade bed.*

Did you hear what I said?

CHARLES *turns to her, speaks with great violence.*

CHARLES

Get out!

*She retreats to the door.*

CHARLES *follows her and slams it.*

*He looks about the room, silent in the moonlight.*

*He sits down and stares at the window.*

## 189.  Interior. Anna's London hotel. Suite. Day. Present.

*A waiter serving a tray of tea. He leaves the room.*

ANNA *in foreground on sofa reading the last few pages of her script of 'The French Lieutenant's Woman'.* DAVID *sitting at a desk, using a calculator and making notes.*

*The phone rings. He picks it up.*

DAVID

Hello

*Silence.*

Hello.

## 190.  Interior. Mike's London house. Day.

MIKE *holding the telephone.*

*Children's voices from the garden.*

DAVID (*voice over*)

Room 206.

MIKE *puts the phone down.*

## 191.  Interior. Anna's hotel. Suite.

DAVID *listening to dialling tone.*

*He replaces the receiver.*

ANNA

Who was that?

DAVID

Don't know. He put the phone down.

ANNA

Who did?

DAVID

I don't know. He didn't say.

ANNA

Maybe it was a wrong number.

DAVID *looks at her.*


**192.    Interior. Mike's London house.**

MIKE *sitting by the phone. In background, in the garden, children are playing.* SONIA *comes into the room. She looks at him.*

SONIA

You all right?

MIKE

What? Yes. Fine.

*She moves to the garden door.*

Listen. What about asking a few people to lunch on Sunday?

SONIA

What people?

MIKE

Oh . . . some of the cast.

SONIA

Fine.

MIKE

Well . . . you know . . . the film's nearly over, Anna's got to get back to the States . . . you know . . .

SONIA

Fine. Fine. As long as it's not the whole unit.

MIKE

No, no, just . . . you know . . .

SONIA

All right. Fine.

*She goes into the garden.*

**193.**   **Interior. Anna's London hotel. Suite.**

*The phone rings.* DAVID *picks it up.*

DAVID

Hello.

MIKE (voice over)

Hello David. It's Mike here. Listen. We're having a little lunch party here on Sunday. Can you both come?

DAVID

Uuh . . . well . . . here's Anna.

*He passes the phone to* ANNA, *his hand over the receiver.*

(*Whispering.*) Lunch on Sunday.

ANNA *lies back on the sofa.*

ANNA (into phone)

Hi!

MIKE (voice over)

You've gone. Where are you? You weren't in your room.

ANNA (laughing)

What?

MIKE (voice over)

In Exeter. Listen, come to lunch on Sunday. Oh, by the way, I love you.

ANNA

How lovely. Yes. We'd love to come. See you then.

MIKE (voice over)

Great.

*She puts the phone down, looks at* DAVID.

ANNA

Lunch on Sunday.

DAVID

I know.

*She picks up her script. He looks at her.*

Weren't you going down to do the last scene on Sunday?

ANNA

No. They're behind schedule. It's Wednesday.

DAVID

Ah. Have they decided what they want to do with the end?

ANNA

I've decided.

DAVID

What have you decided?

ANNA

I want to play it exactly as it's written.

DAVID

Is there going to be a fight about it?

ANNA (*grimly*)

I hope not.


## 194.  Hand holding newspaper.

*The newspaper is opened at an advertisement.*

GRIMES (*voice over*)

'Will Miss Sarah Woodruff urgently communicate her whereabouts to Montague and Montague, 180 Chancery Lane, London.'

Yes. Very well worth it, I would say.


## 195.  Interior. Grimes' office. Day.

GRIMES *and* CHARLES *sit at a desk.*
*On desk various cups with tea dregs, glasses, ashtrays with cigar stubs.*

GRIMES

Well, Mr. Smithson, I'm not going to pretend to you that it will be an easy task. But I have four good men who will go onto the job at once. We shall try the Educational Boards of all the Church Schools. We shall also investigate these new female clerical agencies. They're everywhere, growing like wildfire. And we'll investigate all the girls' academies in London.

CHARLES

Yes.

GRIMES

I shall also be examining the register of deaths.
*Pause.*
One last question, sir, for the moment.

CHARLES

Yes?

GRIMES

Does the young lady wish to be found, would you say, or not?

*Pause.*

CHARLES

I cannot say.

## 196. Interior. Charles' Kensington house. Day.

MONTAGUE *leans back in his chair, reading aloud from a letter.*

MONTAGUE

'We are instructed by Mr. Ernest Freeman, father of Miss Ernestina Freeman, to request you to attend at these chambers at 3 o'clock this coming Friday. Your failure to attend will be regarded as an acknowledgement of our client's right to proceed. Aubrey and Baggott.'

CHARLES

What does it mean?

MONTAGUE

It means they have cold feet. But they're not letting us off altogether. My guess is we will be asked to make a *confessio delicti.*

CHARLES

A statement of guilt?

MONTAGUE

Just so. I am afraid we must anticipate an ugly document. But I can only advise you to sign it. We have no case.

## 197. Exterior. Factory. London. Dusk.

*Dozens of women emerging from the factory.*

CHARLES *stands at a street corner, his eyes searching the crowd. Some of the women look at him and laugh. He turns away.*

## 198. Interior. Aubrey's chambers. Day.

*Piles of legal volumes on the desk and the floor. Box files of cases ranged high around the room.*

CHARLES *and* MONTAGUE *sit side by side opposite a desk.*
AUBREY *is addressing them from behind the desk.*
MR. FREEMAN *stands by the window with his back to the others.*
SERJEANT MURPHY, *a very tall, thin man, stands, arms folded, leaning against a bookcase.*

AUBREY

I now come to your client's sordid liaison with another woman.

*He glowers at* CHARLES.

You may, sir, have thought Mr. Freeman not to be fully cognisant of your amours. You are wrong. We know the name of the female with whom you have entered into such base relations. We have a witness to circumstances I find too disgusting to name. Circumstances which took place in the town of Exeter three months ago, in June of this year.

CHARLES *flushes.* MR. FREEMAN *is now looking at him.*

MURPHY'S *eyes never leave him.*

MONTAGUE

My client did not come here to defend his conduct.

MURPHY

Then you would not defend such an action?

MONTAGUE

With respect, sir, I must reserve judgement on that matter.

MURPHY

The judgement is hardly at issue, Mr. Montague.

AUBREY

Our advice to Mr. Freeman has been clear. In my very long experience this is the vilest example of dishonourable behaviour I have ever had under my survey. I believe firmly that such vicious conduct should be exhibited as a warning to others.

CHARLES *suddenly looks at* MURPHY. *They hold each other's gaze.*

However, it is your client's good fortune that Mr. Freeman has elected to show a mercy the case in no way warrants.

*Pause.*

I have, with esteemed advice – (*He glances at* MURPHY) – prepared an admission of guilt. But I should instruct you that Mr. Freeman's decision not to proceed immediately is contingent upon your client's signing this document in our presence – today.

MURPHY *extends his hand for the document.* AUBREY *passes it to him.*

MURPHY

'I, Charles Henry Smithson, do fully, freely and solely by my desire to declare the truth admit that:
1. I contracted to marry Miss Ernestina Freeman.
2. I was given no cause whatsoever to break my solemn contract with her.
3. I was fully and exactly apprised of her rank in society, her character, her marriage portion, and future prospects, before my engagement to her hand.
4. I did break that contract without any justification whatsoever beyond my own criminal selfishness and lust.
5. I entered into a clandestine liaison with a person named Sarah Woodruff.
6. My conduct throughout this matter has been dishonourable. By it, I have forever forfeited the right to be considered a gentleman.
*Pause.*
I hereby acknowledge that the injured party may make whatever use she desires of this document'.
*Silence.*

MONTAGUE

Mr. Smithson, you are entitled to withdraw with me into another room . . .

CHARLES (*interrupts*)

That will not be necessary.

*He looks at* AUBREY.

But I should like to ask one question. What does 'the injured party may make whatever use she desires of this document' mean?

AUBREY

It means precisely what it says.

MURPHY (*smiling*)

She might for instance wish to have it published in The Times.

CHARLES

And she would be free to do that?

MURPHY

She would indeed.

CHARLES *nods.*

CHARLES

I will sign.

*All stand.* CHARLES *signs the document. He does not wait for the others to follow as he turns and leaves the room.*

199.  **Exterior. London mews. Day. Present.**

*A white Mercedes draws up.* ANNA *jumps out, runs towards the door. The chauffeur gets out, stretches.*

200.  **Interior. Costume shop. Day.**

ANNA *draping a length of material across her. She looks at herself in a long mirror.*

ANNA

Yes, I think I'm going to like her in this.

201.  **Interior. Grimes' office. Day**

GRIMES *and* CHARLES *standing.*

CHARLES

Nothing at all?

GRIMES

Nothing. I am sorry.

*Pause.*

CHARLES

Don't give up.

*He leaves the room.*

202.  **Exterior. Mews. Day. Present.**

ANNA *comes quickly out of the costume shop into the Mercedes. The Mercedes drives off.*

### 203.  Interior. Charles' house. Drawing room. Night.

CHARLES *and* MONTAGUE *sit at a distance from each other.*
*Silence.*

CHARLES
I don't understand. To give herself to me . . . and
then to dismiss me . . . as if I were nothing to her.

MONTAGUE
Perhaps you were nothing to her.
*Pause.*

CHARLES
I cannot believe it.

MONTAGUE
But on the evidence you must believe it.
*Pause.*

CHARLES
No. I do not.


### 204.  Exterior. London street. Night.

CHARLES *walking along the street. He passes a public*
*house. Loud singing from within. He looks through the*
*windows.*


### 205.  Interior. Public house. Night.

CHARLES *comes in and stands, watching. A group of men*
*surround a girl who is dancing on a table. Old ladies, at a*
*table near the window, drinking stout, cackling. A group of*
*young women at the bar.*
CHARLES' *glance swings from one female face to antother.*
*He goes out.*


### 206.  Exterior. London street. Night.

CHARLES *passes a blind beggar, a group of urchins, whores*
*standing in doorways. An old lady, sitting at a window, taps*
*loudly to draw his attention. The whores call out after him.*
*He crosses the street and gets into a hansom cab.*


### 207.  Street off the Haymarket.

*The hansom goes down the street, and turns the corner.*

## 208. Another street.

*This street is narrow and silent.*
*A solitary* GIRL *stands under a gas lamp.*
CHARLES *cranes forward. She has a faint resemblance to*
SARAH. *He knocks with his stick on the roof of the cab. It*
*stops.*
*Footsteps. The* GIRL *looks in the window.*

GIRL

Hullo, sir.


## 209. The girl's house, stairs, and room. Night.

*The* GIRL *leads.* CHARLES *follows.*

GIRL

Is it for all night, sir?

CHARLES

Yes. How much will that be?

GIRL

A sovereign, sir.

*They enter the room. Charles gives her a sovereign.*
Thank you, sir. Make yourself at home. I shan't be a
minute.

*She goes through a door into another room.*
*He stands by the fire.*
*Through the door sounds of a child, a low murmur.*
*The door opens. The* GIRL *comes in.*

It's my little girl, sir. She'll be all right. She's as
good as gold.

*The* GIRL *has undressed and now wears only a peignoir*
*over her naked body.*

I've got some wine, sir. Would you like a glass of
wine?

CHARLES

What wine is it?

GIRL

It's German wine.

CHARLES

Thank you. A glass.

*She goes to a cupboard, takes out a bottle, half empty,*
*and pours a glass, takes it to him.*

90

Sit down by the fire, sir, go on, for a minute, warm yourself. I'll see if I can get it going better.

*He sits, with glass. She kneels at his feet and pokes the fire.*

It's best quality coal, but it's the cellar. It's so damp down there.

CHARLES *looks at her breasts. He swallows wine and grimaces. The* GIRL *stops poking the fire.*

That's got a bit more life to it.

*She stands.*

Like the wine, sir? Go on, have some more.

*The baby begins to cry in the other room.*

*The* GIRL *pours some more wine.*

Drink up. It's good for your muscles.

*The cries grow louder. The* GIRL *stands uncertainly.*

CHARLES

Go to her.

GIRL

Yes, I'll just . . .

*She goes into the other room. The door remains open.*
CHARLES *drinks. Sounds of* GIRL *attempting to soothe the baby. The baby is not soothed.*

*The* GIRL *comes back into the room. She sits, pulls on some boots.*

GIRL

I can't quieten her. I've got a friend – next door. She'll take her. Oh, I'm sorry, sir.

*She stands, puts on cloak over her peignoir.*

Could you just . . . keep an eye on her, sir . . . for a minute?

CHARLES

Yes, yes.

GIRL

I won't be a minute.

*She goes out.*

CHARLES *sits with drink. A moment's silence from the other room, then a prolonged cry.* CHARLES *stands, goes to the open door and looks into the room.*

91

**210. Other room.**

*In dim light, the baby in a small truckle bed.*

CHARLES

Hush, hush. Your mother will return soon.

*At this the child screams.* CHARLES *goes to her, pats her head. This has no effect. He suddenly gropes for his watch, frees the chain from his waistcoat and dangles it over her. The cries stop. She reaches up, grabs the watch. She plays with it. He gently takes it from her and dangles it in front of her, like a pendulum. She watches this with delight, then grabs it, gurgling with laughter.*

CHARLES

Yes, yes, isn't it a pretty watch? . . . That's a good little girl . . . isn't it a pretty watch?

*The door of the other room opens. The* GIRL *comes through and stands in the doorway.*

GIRL

She wasn't there.

*She looks at the gurgling baby and then at* CHARLES.
Oh . . .


**211. Close up. Baby with watch.**

**212. Sitting room.**

CHARLES *walks in, drains his glass, grimaces.*
*The* GIRL *comes in from the other room, closing the door. She slips out of her boots and cloak.*

GIRL

You like little baby girls, sir?

CHARLES *grunts.*

Would you like me to sit on your lap?

CHARLES

Do.

*The* GIRL *does.*

GIRL

You're a very handsome gentleman.

CHARLES

You're a very pretty girl.

You like us wicked girls? You like wickedness, do you?

*She slips his hand under her peignoir onto her breasts. She kisses him. His hand wanders over her body. Her robe falls away. She stands.*

Come on. It's a nice soft bed.

*He stands. She drops her robe, shows him her body.*

GIRL

Like me?

*The baby begins to cry in the other room.*

*The GIRL gets into the bed. He suddenly sways, closes his eyes, puts his hand to his head.*

GIRL

You all right?

*The baby continues to cry. He walks to the bed and looks down at the GIRL.*

CHARLES

I don't know your name.

GIRL

Sarah. What's yours?

*He is racked by a sudden spasm.*

GIRL

What's the matter?

*The GIRL jumps out of bed. She puts her hand on his shoulder.*

CHARLES *(violently)*

Go to your baby!

*He rushes from the room.*

## 213.   Exterior. House. Alley. Long shot.

CHARLES *vomiting.*

## 214.   Exterior. Victorian house. Day. Present.

*The house is double fronted, with a portico.*

*The door opens, suddenly. A GIRL of nine stands in the doorway. She looks down the steps.*

GIRL

Hullo! I saw you through the window!

**215.  Reverse shot.**

ANNA *and* DAVID *walking up the steps of the house.*

> ANNA
>
> Hullo! Are you Lizzie?
>
> LIZZIE
>
> Yes. I am.

**216.  Mike's house. The garden.**

*Food and drink on tables.*

*In the background* SONIA *talking to* DAVID, 'GROGAN' *to* 'ERNESTINA', MIKE *to* 'SAM'.

'MRS. POULTENEY' *and* ANNA.

> 'MRS. POULTENEY'
>
> I must say they have a lovely garden, don't they?
>
> ANNA
>
> Yes.
>
> 'MRS. POULTENEY'
>
> Well, it's a lovely house. Don't you think? So serene. Of course, she seems so serene, doesn't she, the wife?
>
> ANNA
>
> Mmn. Yes.
>
> 'MRS. POULTENEY'
>
> Look at their little girl. Isn't she lovely? Such a pretty little thing.
>
> LIZZIE *passes.* 'MRS. POULTENEY' *stops her.*
>
> Aren't you a pretty little thing? Who made that dress for you?
>
> LIZZIE
>
> I don't know.
>
> 'MRS. POULTENEY' (*to* ANNA)
>
> I made all my own dresses once upon a time. Everyone admired them. I honestly have no idea why I took up acting.

**217.  Another part of the garden.**

MIKE *and* DAVID.

> DAVID
>
> Have they decided how they are going to end it?

MIKE

End it?

DAVID

I hear they keep changing the script.

MIKE

Not at all. Where did you hear that?

DAVID

Well, there are two endings in the book, aren't there? A happy ending and an unhappy ending?

MIKE

Yes. We're going for the first ending – I mean the second ending.

DAVID

Which one is that?

MIKE

Hasn't Anna told you?


**218.   Interior. Mike's house.**

'SAM' and 'ERNESTINA' *playing a duet on the piano.*


**219.   Another part of the garden.**

ANNA *and* SONIA.

ANNA

It's a great garden. Who looks after it for you?

SONIA

I do.

ANNA

What, all on your own?

SONIA

Mmn. More or less.

ANNA

What about Mike? Doesn't he help?

SONIA

Oh, when he's here. A bit. He's pretty lazy actually.
    ANNA *smiles.*

ANNA

I really envy you.

SONIA

Envy me? Why?

95

ANNA

Well, for being able to create such a lovely garden.

SONIA (*laughing*)

Oh, I wouldn't bother to envy me, if I were you. Have some more wine.

*SONIA goes towards a table for a bottle.*


**220.   Interior. Mike's house. Landing.**

*MIKE rushing up stairs.*
*The bathroom door opens.*
*ANNA comes out, wearing a coat.*
*He grasps her arm, speaks in a low voice.*

MIKE

This is pure bloody hell.

ANNA

For Christ's sake! Anyone could . . .

MIKE

We've got to talk. Properly. At Windermere.

ANNA

What are we going to say?

MIKE

We've got to decide – what we want.

ANNA

Yes. Yes.

*Voice of SONIA from below:*

SONIA

I think she's getting her coat.

*ANNA breaks away, looks down.*
*SONIA, DAVID and LIZZIE looking up from the hall.*

ANNA

Coming!

*She turns to MIKE and kisses him on the cheek.*

See you at Windermere.

*She goes down the stairs to DAVID and SONIA. LIZZIE opens the front door. They walk towards it.*


**221.   Close shot. Mike.**

*Voices over:*

ANNA

It's been a lovely afternoon. I've had a great time. It's such a beautiful house.

SONIA

Thank you.

DAVID

Very good to meet you.

SONIA

And you. (*To* ANNA.)
Good luck for the last scene.

ANNA (*laughing*)

We'll need it.
*The door closes.*

**222.  Exterior. Hotel garden. Day.**

*The following title appears on the screen.*
SOME YEARS LATER
CHARLES, *with a beard, walks along the terrace of a hotel by the sea. He sits down.*
*A porter descends the steps of the hotel and gives* CHARLES *a telegram. He opens it.*

**223.  The telegram.**

'She is found. Under name Mrs. Roughwood. Montague.'

**224.  Exterior. Lake Windermere. Day.**

*Calm water.*
*A small steam-powered vessel is puffing slowly across the lake.*
CHARLES, *bearded and gaunt, sits in the prow searching for something on land. He raises his pocket telescope to his eye.*

**225.  Exterior. Lake. Charles' eye line.**

*High above the shore stands a white house with bow windows and green slate roof.*

**226.  Close up. Charles.**

*His interest quickens. He pulls a note out of his pocket.*

## 227. The note.

"MRS. ROUGHWOOD"
THE NEW HOUSE
WINDERMERE

## 228. Lake shore. Day.

CHARLES *ascending a wooded bank. Behind him, the lake.*
*Piano music.*
CHARLES *looks through shrubbery at the white house.*
*He begins to skirt it. He waits for signs of life.*

## 229. The New House. Day.

CHARLES' *view – a glimpse of white walls through dense*
*shrubbery.*
*The sound of playing children.*

## 230. New House. Day.

CHARLES *cautiously circles the house from a distance. He*
*reaches a lawn, at a higher level above the house.*
*The house comes into full view.*
CHARLES *approaches it.*

## 231. Exterior. The house.

CHARLES *knocks at front door, waits.*
*The door is opened by a* BOY *of twelve.*

> BOY

Good morning.

> CHARLES

Good morning.

> BOY

I'm Tom Elliott. Who are you?

> CHARLES

My name is Smithson.

> BOY

Mama and Papa are abroad.

> CHARLES

I . . . I'm looking for a Mrs. Roughwood.

> BOY

Oh! Yes. Please come in.

CHARLES *goes in.*

## 232.  Interior. House.

*The interior of the house is white, full of light. A piano is playing, haltingly. Laughter from another room.*
*The* BOY *goes to the foot of the stairs and shouts up.*

BOY

Mrs. Roughwood! Someone to see you.

*The* BOY *turns to* CHARLES.

I think she's working. But she doesn't mind being interrupted.

SARAH's *voice from above: 'What is it?'*
*She appears on the landing and looks down into the hall.*
*She sees* CHARLES.
*He stands still, looking at her.*

BOY

Please go up,

CHARLES *walks up the stairs towards her. She waits.*
*He reaches her. They look at each other.*
*She turns, goes towards room. He follows.*

## 233.  Interior. Studio.

*Pictures on walls. A trestle table. Piles of drawings. A drawing in progress on a small table.*
*She closes the door.*

CHARLES

Mrs. Roughwood.

SARAH

Mr. Smithson.
*Pause.*

CHARLES

My solicitor was told you lived at this address. I do not know by whom.

SARAH

By me.
*Pause.*

CHARLES

By you?
*Pause.*

I have been looking for you for three years.
*Pause.*

99

I broke off my engagement. I came back for you, to take you with me, to marry you. You had gone.

*Pause.*

And now . . . all these years later . . . you choose to let me know that you are alive. Why?

SARAH

I could not do so before this.

*Pause.*

CHARLES

You have married.

SARAH

No. I have not. I pass as a widow . . . in the world.

*Pause.*

CHARLES

What is this house?

SARAH

He is an architect. His name is Elliott. They gave me shelter – a long time ago. I am tutor to their children, but I . . . I am free to do my own work. They have encouraged it.

*He looks at the drawings. They are of children.*

CHARLES

These are yours?

SARAH

Yes.

CHARLES

You have found your gift.

*He looks at her.*

Why did you leave Exeter? You told me you loved me. You showed . . . your love.

*Pause.*

Answer me.

SARAH

There was a madness in me . . . at the time, a bitterness, an envy. I forced myself on you, knowing that you had . . . other obligations. It was unworthy. I suddenly saw, after you had gone, that I had to destroy what had begun between us.

CHARLES

Are you saying you never loved me?

100

SARAH

I could not say that.

CHARLES

But you must say that! You must say: 'I am totally
evil. I used him as an instrument. I do not care that
in all this time he has not seen a woman to compare
with me, that his life has been a desert without me,
that he has sacrificed everything. . . for me!' Say it!

SARAH

No.

CHARLES

Why did you ask me here? What do you want of
me?

SARAH

I saw the newspaper advertisements long ago –

CHARLES

You *saw* them? You *read* them? And did nothing?

SARAH

Yes. I changed my name.

CHARLES

Then you have not only caused my ruin. You have
taken pleasure in doing so.

SARAH

You misjudge me. It has taken me this time to find
my own life. It has taken me this time . . . to find
my freedom.

CHARLES

Freedom!

SARAH

Yes.

CHARLES

To make a mockery of love, of all human feeling. Is
that all Exeter meant to you?
One brief transaction of the flesh? Only that? You
have planted a dagger in me and your 'damned
freedom' gives you licence to twist it in my heart.
Well, no more!

*He strides to the door. She seizes his arm.*

SARAH

No!

*He flings her away, violently.*

CHARLES

Yes!

*She falls to the floor, hitting her head. He stops.*
*She sits up, holding her head. He stares down at her.*
*She looks at him. She smiles.*

SARAH

Mr. Smithson . . . I called you here . . . to ask your
forgiveness.

*Pause.*

You loved me once.

*Pause.*

If you still love me, you can forgive me.

*She stands.*

I know it is your perfect right to damn me.

*Pause.*

But if you do . . . still . . . love me . . .

*They look into each others' eyes.*

CHARLES

Then I must . . . forgive you.

*Pause.*

SARAH

Yes. You must.

*A piano is heard.*
*Sunlight falls across the room.*
CHARLES *and* SARAH *moves towards each other.*
*The camera tracks closer and stops.*
*They are embracing.*
*They kiss.*

CHARLES (softly)

Sarah.

*Slow dissolve to:*


**234.   Exterior. Lake boathouse. Evening.**

*A rowing boat is emerging from the darkness of a boathouse
on to the lake.* SARAH *sits in the prow,* CHARLES *is by the
oars.*

*As the boat glides out into the calm evening water* CHARLES
*begins to row slowly.*

*Rock music.*

**235. Exterior. The New House garden. Night. Present.**
*The unit party in full swing. A three-piece band on a plat-*
*form. All the actors we have seen in the film are present, in*
*modern clothes, apart from* MIKE *and* ANNA, *who still wear*
*their costumes of the previous scene.*
'GROGAN' *lurches by, drunk, dancing with* 'MARY'. 'SAM' *is*
*dancing with* 'MRS. POULTENEY'; *the* 'PROSTITUTE' *with* 'MR.
FREEMAN'; 'MRS. FAIRLEY' *with* 'SERJEANT MURPHY'; 'AUNT
TRANTER' *with* 'MR. AUBREY'; *the* 'DAIRYWOMAN' *with* 'MON-
TAGUE'; 'MRS. ENDICOTT' *with* 'SIR TOM'. 'NAT', *the* 'DAIRYMAN'
*and members of the crew stand around.* ANNA *is dancing*
*with a member of the crew.* MIKE *is standing aside, drinking.*

**236. Close up. Mike.**
*He looks at his watch, signals to* ANNA.

**237. Close up. Anna.**
*She responds to* MIKE's *signal, kisses her partner on the*
*cheek, turns.*

**238. The party. Long shot.**
ANNA *walking towards the house.*
'ERNESTINA' *comes into the garden, wearing a fur coat, and*
*boots. She goes up on a small platform, opens her coat and,*
*to applause and whistling, reveals that she is dressed in a*
*Victorian corset. She starts to do a kind of fan dance, open-*
*ing and closing her coat. Great enthusiasm.*

**239. Interior. The New House. Anna's dressing room.**
ANNA *at her dressing table.*
*She has changed her clothes.*
*She stares at herself in the mirror.*

**240.  The party.**
MIKE *moves towards the house. He is stopped by the* 'PROSTI-TUTE' *who kisses him, and then by* 'GROGAN', *who hugs him. In background* 'ERNESTINA' *being carried off the platform. Laughter. She is thrown about between a number of men, who dance with her in turn.*

**241.  Interior. New House.**
MIKE *runs into the hall and up the stairs on which he first saw* 'Mrs. Roughwood'.

**242.  Anna's dressing room. Empty.**
MIKE *rushes in. The room is empty.*
*Sarah's long red wig hangs from a block.*
*He quickly opens another door, which leads into the white room.*

**243.  Interior. The white room.**
*Moonlight falls across the room.*
*Sounds of the party from below. Suddenly the sound of a car starting up.* MIKE *runs to the window, looks out.*

**244.  Exterior. House.**
ANNA'S *white car driving towards the gate.*

**245.  Exterior. House. Window.**
MIKE *at window. He calls out:*

MIKE

Sarah!